GODBEARING

Godbearing

evangelism reconceived

Elaine A. Robinson

The Pilgrim Press
Cleveland

for **ED BECK**

The Pilgrim Press, 700 Prospect Avenue, Cleveland, Ohio 44115-1100
thepilgrimpress.com

Printed in the United States of America on acid-free paper

09 08 07 06 05 5 4 3 2 1

Library of Congress Cataloging-in-Publication Data

Robinson, Elaine A., 1959–
Godbearing : evangelism reconceived / Elaine A. Robinson.
p. cm.
Includes bibliographical references and index.
ISBN-13 : 978-0-8298-1708-9
1. Witness bearing (Christianity) I. Title.

BV4520.R642 2006
269'.2—dc22 2006017773

ISBN-13 : 978-0-8298-1708-9
ISBN-10 : 0-8298-1708-5

contents

Foreword *vii*
Acknowledgments *ix*
Introduction *1*

one **THE SPIRIT OF OUR TIMES** *5*
The Decline of the U.S. Church *5*
The Temptation Scene Today *9*
Reconnecting with the Spirit of Life *32*

two **WHY "EVANGELISM" ISN'T THE ANSWER** *38*
Evangelism Is Not Evangelicalism *41*
Where in the Bible Is Evangelism? *58*
The Content of the Gospel: Radical Relationship *63*
A Brief History of "Evangelism" *67*

three **JESUS, THE PROTOTYPICAL GODBEARER** *76*
The Christ Character and the Radical Relationality of God *77*
The Witnesses of Scripture *84*
Witnessing Jesus as Godbearer *89*

four **FOLLOWING JESUS** *113*
Mary, *Theotokos*, Godbearer *113*
Mary Magdalene, Apostle to the Apostles, Godbearer *119*
Paul, Apostle to the Gentiles, Godbearer *124*
Bartolomé de Las Casas, Godbearer *131*
Rosa Parks, Godbearer *135*

five **OPENING AGAIN TO LIFE** *140*
Openness to the Word *143*
Openness to Living on the Edge of the Raft *146*
Openness to the Future *148*
Becoming a New Creation in Christ *150*

Notes *153*
Index of Authors and Subjects *163*
Index of Scripture *165*

foreword

It is a matter of continual debate in the academy whether evangelism should be considered an academic discipline, but two things are certain: 1) The varied practices of evangelism are widely spread in mainline and more evangelically defined denominations as well as independent church and parachurch organizations. 2) The integrity of the varied practices is widely disputed, and there is little or no agreement across party lines whether evangelism should proliferate or diminish. This is the nexus point at which Dr. Robinson's timely book enters the fray. She recognizes that mainline churches are concerned about loss of membership and influence in society, and she rightly points out that their engagement in evangelistic practices is often out of numerical pragmatic concern. At the same time, she is aware that pure pragmatism is not a good reason for the church to engage specific ecclesial practices. There must always be a biblical and theological basis for the church's acts of ministry and mission.

North America is a very individualistic society, and to a large extent our churches are consumer oriented and individual-centered. Dr. Robinson accurately points out that those who proudly carry the label of evangelist are often unwitting advocates of a culture that is in basic conflict with God's view of the world as reflected in the New Testament. In this context she underscores that the gospel of Jesus Christ is highly personal as well as communal. She recognizes that personal and individualistic are not the same thing, and she is calling God's church to a communal understanding of the gospel as radical relationship with the prototypical Godbearer—Jesus Christ: "Thus, saying yes to Jesus Christ does not consist in a moment's ecstasy, but in a lifetime of turning toward relationship and away from brokenness." Rather than being about me as an individual, this personal Godbearing as a way of living is a "revolutionary, subversive power of grace forming the Christ character within us and overflowing into the world in radically relational ways. No longer focused upon the standards of society that urge us to be the first, best, most, least, or lowest as a sign of favored status or blessing, we live radically related to God, self, others and the whole creation."

The pages that follow are a clarion call to all God's people, that our faithfulness requires us to open ourselves to the scriptural understanding of Godbearing as an ongoing response to God's grace. Invoking Joshua 24:15–23, she reminds us to "choose this day whom you will serve." And this acceptance is not a single, solitary decision: "Indeed, accepting faith in Christ means renouncing identity as a purely individual reality. By faith, we become part of [God's] larger reality, woven into the fabric of creation in which the harmony and radical relationship of God are the very sinews that hold us and move us." From judiciously chosen examples that stretch from Mary Magdalene and the Apostle Paul to Bartolomé de Las Casas and Rosa Parks, the reader is provided a window into the practical dimensions of personal Godbearing in the world.

Evangelism will remain a contested word, but evangelism will be a less feared and contested practice if we take the message of this book to heart and let its wisdom inform our ecclesial practices.

—*W. Stephen Gunter*

acknowledgments

Many people have contributed to this project in one way or another. First, I'm delighted to have worked with my tried and true editor, Ulrike Guthrie, and the team at The Pilgrim Press. They've guided this book from its conception in 2005, when I was invited to travel weekly from Fort Worth to Dallas to teach a course in evangelism at Perkins School of Theology. Because the seeds of *Godbearing* were planted during that semester as an adjunct professor, I am indebted to my friend and colleague, Marjorie Procter-Smith, who first suggested I teach the course and encouraged me to develop a new approach to the subject. I'm also grateful to the twenty-five Perkins students who dared to take my class and to engage in conversation around this subject.

My graduate assistant, Krister White, proofread chapters, provided thoughtful insights, and conducted research for this manuscript. He is an excellent scholar in his own right and facilitated my writing on many occasions. Two colleagues and mentors, both exemplary scholars, read portions of this book in various stages of development: my sincere thanks to Joerg Rieger and Lyn Osiek, who took the time to provide constructive criticism and helpful comments. Any errors or lapses that remain within the text are due entirely to the author's shortcomings.

The support of Brite colleagues over the past several years—especially David Balch, Stacey Floyd-Thomas, Joey Jeter, Leo Perdue, and Mark Toulouse—has provided me with an oasis for which I continue to be deeply grateful.

And to my best friend, Shawn Link, thanks for sharing this journey with me and with Ethan, Henry, and Mimi.

introduction

Some twenty years ago when I was a young Air Force officer living in the high desert of Southern California, one of my neighbors invited me to dinner. Over ravioli and Chianti, Joe—a sixtyish ex-"Mafia" man turned Pentecostal preacher, the author of a tell-all paperback to verify his story—opened his Bible to share with me the good news of Jesus Christ. Then he prayed for me to receive the Holy Spirit. Although I was unchurched at the time, I possessed a deep, lifelong yearning to know and experience God, to believe in the reality of God with all my heart, mind, soul, and strength. As a child, I had known God, though my family had shunned religious belief and practice. In a very real sense, I was not "unconnected," but "unchurched." I lacked a community and tradition that could offer formation, accountability, and growth in faith.

Yet, I never took up Joe's offer to attend his church, and we never again broke bread together. Something about the encounter was off-putting. Despite my longing to believe and belong, I was uncomfortable and unsettled by Joe's attempt to "evangelize" me. I wanted what he claimed to offer, but I was unconvinced of the reality of which he spoke or by the words and approach he used.

I suspect my first encounter with being "evangelized" is not entirely unlike that experienced by countless other unchurched persons. While something deep within the human being yearns to be grasped by the reality of God in Christ in the Holy Spirit—the divine, the spiritual realm—a certain skepticism and discomfort, perhaps even suspicion about the motives of the evangelist push us away. The fact that most Protestant denominations in the United

States are experiencing a decline in numbers suggests that we should reach out to those who are unchurched or unconnected and that the renewal of the church is of vital concern.[1] The fact that many Christians do find meaning and significance in their faith suggests that others can also live in and out of this reality. But the approach taken by Joe twenty years ago continues to cause Christians and others to feel uncomfortable, wary, and skeptical.

A few years ago, as an ordained minister and academic theologian, I was invited to participate in a denominational summit on evangelism in Havana, Cuba, bringing together church leaders from throughout the Americas and the Caribbean. Over the two weeks, we delegates worshipped, ate, prayed, consulted, cried, and celebrated together. We were often deeply moved by the stories of delegates from Mexico, Cuba, Brazil, Guatemala, and other countries. Yet, the leadership of the summit—all from the United States—displayed a level of paternalism, as well as a desire to convey the "American way of life," that I thought, naively, had long since gone out of favor.

On the second to last day, in perhaps the most telling moment of the summit, one of the leaders invited a North American to share his personal witness during a plenary session. He was a retired physician and university professor whose story included references to playing golf at the country club and having access to the best medical care in the United States. He concluded by sharing the good news that his son had secured a lucrative job working with computers after having recovered from a devastating and life-changing injury. The Latin Americans listened politely to the interpreter's translation of his well-intentioned but misdirected testimony.

Amilcar from Guatemala then rose to share his witness. He spoke about the widespread violence and poverty in his home country, the lack of any salary for pastors, his own conversion experience while staring at the barrel of a rifle as the guerrillas shot and killed the friend who was standing beside him, his lifelong volunteer work for the church, and his hope in the possibility of transformation in this world. By the time Amilcar finished speaking, there was not a dry eye or an unmoved heart in the room. The contrast between the privileged life of the North American and the struggle against poverty, violence, and despair in Central America was a powerful reminder that the gospel message is as needed in our world as ever—not only to bring hope to those who despair, but also to break the systems of oppression, power, and privilege that undermine the life and well-being of so many peoples around the world. To be connected to God in Christ in the Holy Spirit and to a community of faith is to move into radical relationality and seek the flourishing of all life. The work of God in the world is not yet finished.

Despite the moments when I have experienced the failures of human beings, including myself, I believe in God in Christ in the Holy Spirit. I believe in the church and its message of abundant life. I believe that the reality of God is breaking into our world even in the midst of our post-Enlightenment, postmodern society. But like many others in the church today I simply do not feel at home in the world constructed, inhabited, and projected by contemporary evangelists. Something about the methods, the means, the language, the imagery, and the theology of traditional evangelism is off-putting. Well-meaning people of faith are confronted with a constant theological danger: the Word of life can be distorted and destructive when placed in the hands of human beings. Yet there remains the constant hope that the promises and the reality of God cannot be compromised. God in Christ in the Holy Spirit works in and through us, in spite of who we are from moment to moment.

This book is a journey into and recovery from the discomfort I felt in my twenties as an unchurched (yet connected) person and that I feel today as a minister and theologian. It is about the disorienting and reorienting process of life in God. I am convinced it is a journey that countless other Christians share. There are many books written on the practices of evangelism, some on the biblical foundations, and a few on a theology of evangelism. Most of the books to date have been written by men, and only a few of those by men of color. Few of the writings on evangelism stray far from the beaten path and fewer still seek new ways of engaging and challenging the subject. Indeed, many persons have lamented the lack of genuine dialogue, critical inquiry, and varying perspectives within the "field" of evangelism. While I do not claim to present the "right" way to approach the subject, since we all see "in a mirror dimly," I do suggest that we need new and critical ways of expressing our theology and practices of evangelization within the contemporary, multicultural society of the United States and, in turn, in relation to other peoples and cultures. In a word, we need to reconceive this important work as Godbearing. In the following chapters, we will explore and develop the practice of Godbearing as a primary calling of all who follow Christ.

one THE SPIRIT OF OUR TIMES

In this chapter, we begin the work of reconceiving evangelism as Godbearing. Because we live in an intellectual and theological age that recognizes the inescapably historical and cultural nature of human life, we are compelled, initially, to trace the spirit of our times. First, the decline of Christian faith in North America has been a growing concern since the 1960s. When we consider our society and churches, we become aware of the "prevailing culture of one or infinity," as it is fueled by the social impulses toward consumption, individualism, and imperialism. These impulses have pushed the Spirit of Life to the margins of our existence, even as the rhetoric of the United States purports to speak of God and faith. Thus, our first task is to take a hard look at the situation confronting contemporary Christianity in the United States. Only with this awareness in place can we begin to choose the narrow, sometimes difficult, sometimes risky way of Godbearing.

THE DECLINE OF THE U.S. CHURCH

For many mainline denominations in the United States today, the image of withering or decay is appropriate. Sometime around the mid-1960s, the mainline Protestant churches reversed direction and began a decades-long decline. "By 1990 these denominations had lost between one-fifth and one-third of the membership they claimed in 1965 and the proportion of Americans affiliated with them had reached a twentieth century low."[1] While the United States remains one of the most religiously expressive countries in the developed world, the future of mainline Protestantism is uncertain, shrouded in shadows. If the trend continues, the United States seems poised to follow the path of Western Europe toward an increasingly secularized and religiously apathetic society. There exists a gnawing sense that Christianity in the developed, Western world is dispirited, lacking vitality, struggling to stay awake. While philosophers might argue that this is the natural outcome of the ongoing process of the Enlightenment, the Christian narrative resists this explanation, as do most contemporary sociologists, given that belief in God remains widespread in the United States. So the church searches for answers and seeks new life.

In some circles, the answer to the decline of the Christian faith in North America is obvious and straightforward: evangelism.[2] Lyle Schaller, who has made a career of analyzing the church and creating strategies for its renewal, argues in his latest missive that the turnaround of the mainline churches will require "radical changes . . . including moving evangelism and missions to the top of the agenda."[3] Church after church, denomination after denomination turns to this murky messiah as the best hope for renewal. Book after book offers hope through marketing methods, church growth techniques, small group ministries, megachurch models, seeker services, and a cornucopia of evangelistic springs of new life. While not the savior of the world, evangelism might just be the savior of the church; at the very least, it seems to offer a way to illuminate and reenlighten life together.

Yet, as with any penultimate reality, evangelism cannot bring the ultimate—the reality of God—into our midst. Indeed, evangelism is a practice that too often fails to provide more than the fractured light scattered about by a prism. The language of renewal and life in God flows like a river, but the lived expression of this faith often pools like stagnant water. To use another metaphor, we might say that contemporary evangelism tries to put a band-aid on a broken leg or a broken heart: It provides the appearance of attending to the wound, while ignoring the deeper symptoms and difficulties facing the patient. The answer to the decline of Christian faith in the United States lies not in more and better methods; nor is it found in sheer numerical growth. It is not even found in the megachurches overflowing with purpose-driven people who want their best life now. The answer lies only in the reality of God in Christ in the Holy

Spirit. The living God continues to be faithful to the covenant of life, even as the churches in North America find themselves captivated by the lure of the surrounding culture, the culture of one or infinity, which craves the extremes.

While there is general agreement that—with the exception of the mostly evangelical megachurches—the church in the United States is in decline, explaining this trend is fraught with difficulty. Some attribute the decline to outdated worship services or theologically laden messages, and this is precisely one of the selling points for many megachurches today. Saddleback Church in California, Willow Creek in Illinois, and Houston's Lakewood Church in part attribute their success in attracting "seekers" to their emphasis on making unchurched persons feel "comfortable." Before building his 7,200-seat sanctuary, Bill Hybels of Willow Creek conducted market research, which indicated that "traditional symbols would scare away non-churchgoers."[4] Thus, at Willow Creek their multimillion dollar sanctuary has no crosses, stained glass, wooden pews, or hymnals, but plenty of entertainment and good, clean fun. Performance is the word of the day: they "are not just competing with other denominations, but with all other forms of entertainment, especially television."[5] As the executive director of Joel Osteen's Lakewood Church has said of the design of their new facility, the former arena of the Houston Rockets, "We really want it to feel like a concert."[6] With its stadium seating for sixteen thousand people, thirty-foot waterfalls, and supersized video screens, no doubt it does.

Moreover, in general, the megachurches shy away from deeply theological considerations, instead focusing on positive, upbeat messages related to living the good life—what is often considered to be a "prosperity gospel." The contents page of Joel Osteen's *Your Best Life Now* lists seven major parts, none of which mention God, Jesus Christ, or the Holy Spirit. While God does appear in several chapter titles, Osteen's theological vision also includes such claims as: "Enlarge Your Vision," which sounds suspiciously like the Prayer of Jabez that urged us to enlarge our territory, "God has More in Store!" and "Choosing Right Thoughts." As Osteen explained to Larry King in a June 2005 interview, his message is a simple one, encouraging people to get away from negative thoughts and to claim the good life that God wants them to have now. After all, he notes, the gospel is good news, and he simply tries to preach "practical principles."[7] In a similar vein, in their study of Saddleback Church, Putnam and Feldstein describe Rick Warren preaching a series of "messages on 'God's principles for life's common situations,'" the first of which is entitled, "What to Do When You're Overwhelmed."[8] A faithful member of Warren's flock explains the appeal, saying that in the Lutheran Church of his youth, he "couldn't make the translation . . . I never got the connection between church and God being part of everyday life." But at Saddleback Church, "the teaching was so practical and easy to understand."[9] Thus, in this approach to church renewal, analysts argue that traditional theology must be recast in more marketable and palatable terms. The church needs to loosen up and lighten up.

On the other side of the debate, there are analysts who argue that the decline is attributable to theological liberalism, which "is not an empowering system of belief but rather a set of conjectures concerning religious matters. It supports honesty and other moral virtues, and it encourages tolerance and civility in a pluralistic society, but it does not inspire the kind of conviction that creates strong religious communities." [10] In this view, the mainline denominations have a liberal bias that resists clear theological teachings and is based in ethical concerns. Here we find the claim that a more open and progressive theological perspective has "reduced the Christian faith to belief in God and respect for Jesus and the Golden Rule, and among this group a growing proportion have little need for the church."[11] William Abraham's proposal in *The Logic of Evangelism* for returning to a rigorous catechetical instruction represents a variation on this theme.[12] In this version of what ails the church, reclaiming a strong, hierarchical theology and ecclesiology is the way forward. The church needs to tighten the reins and get serious again.

Yet, whether calling for less theological substance or more, for fewer traditional trappings or a return to them, for reducing church structures or reinforcing them, these and other analysts of church decline seldom attend to the larger reality of life in the United States and its impact on the Christian faith. Specifically, the rise of consumerism, individualism, and imperialism over the past fifty years or so has radically altered the landscape of life in the United States and infected communities of faith, undermining our spiritual health. Are megachurches and their market-oriented, "simplified" theology the future of Christian faith? Is a return to that old-time religion with its insistence on catechesis the answer? When we probe more deeply into the contemporary context, we find that neither approach can resolve what ails us, due to a larger process of erosion that contributes to a subtle distortion of the faith, whether mainline or megachurch. Renewal begins with a return to the biblical witnesses and the disorienting, uncomfortable message of the gospel of Jesus as it confronts us with our brokenness and lovelessness and brings to light the diminishment of life together as the body of Christ in the world.

THE TEMPTATION SCENE TODAY

To understand the contemporary context and the problem it poses for the church today, we turn first to Matthew 4:1–11 (cf. Luke 4:1–13), the temptation of Jesus by the devil, as a basis for reflection. This scene follows immediately upon Jesus' baptism, at the beginning of his ministry or his visible life lived in and for God. Jesus is led by the Spirit into this deserted place where he is confronted with the possibility of turning away from God. Notably, this "testing" occurs not before, but after Jesus has publicly declared his commitment to serving God's way. Alone in the wilderness, fasting and praying, Jesus is presented with three temptations: 1) turning stones into bread; 2) throwing himself down from the pinnacle of the temple, unharmed; and 3) ruling all the kingdoms of the world. While there are several possible interpretations of these temptations, in our context we can understand them as representing the desire for material goods, the desire for immortality or to be infinite, and the desire to rule all earthly peoples. Jesus of Nazareth who is the Christ rejects each of these penultimate realities and points toward God as the ultimate reality and the way that leads to the fullness of life. One cannot love and serve God, one cannot see the way of God, if one is caught in the grip of any of these idolatrous temptations. Enamored with the lesser loves, we lose our direction toward Love itself.

Too often we have viewed this biblical passage either as a glimpse of Jesus' obedience and sinlessness in the face of temptation or as a lesson for our personal, individual lives in God. But what we need to grasp is its larger social vision and the message for our situation today. In the context of U.S. society in the twenty-first century, Matthew 4 enables us to see the decline of the churches in terms of our social, economic, political, and institutional preferences for the penultimate over the reality of God. Indeed, this passage illuminates that traditional mainline denominations and evangelical megachurches alike are in a state of decline, for life in God is a spiritual reality with specific contours and not a function of numbers. The gospel does not point us toward a life of achievement and accumulation; it does not point toward status and power; it does not even point toward upward spiraling happiness and ecstatic experiences. The gospel points us toward God. It does not weave us more successfully into the social fabric, but renews the very fabric of our lives in God and weaves us more deeply into the web of creation. Understanding that our churches in North America are enamored with playing the numbers' game, counting members like the pennies in a piggy bank, enables us to better grasp the logic and basis of decline.

The Impulse Toward One or Infinity

The numbers' game in today's churches can be described most succinctly in terms of the impulse toward one or infinity. In the numerical reality of "one," we find singularity and uniqueness. Slogans such as "we're number one" and "one of a kind" pervade contemporary society. Advertising hails "an army of one" and "the power of one." It regales us with the virtues of one calorie servings; touts the goodness of consolidating services or debt on one bill; proclaims that this company or that product is number one in sales, consumer confidence, or taste tests. To be known by one name is to be at the top of one's game: Oprah, Trump, Hilfiger, Dubya, Ellen, Tiger, Shaq. We are drawn to oneness. It signifies winning. It gives us hope.

At the other end of the spectrum, though related to one, is infinity, the mathematical and philosophical concept of limitlessness.[13] It is a numberless number that eludes our grasp. Moreover, infinities "come in two sizes . . . not only the infinitely large but also the infinitely small."[14] We long for the extremes. Today, not only is more considered better, but less is too, and sometimes more and less are simultaneously better. At one end of the spectrum, we seek the biggest, the best, the most extreme of objects or experiences. It appears perfectly reasonable to spend ten million dollars or more for one tourist to ride in space; after all, he earned the money. Our fifty-inch LCD HDTV adorns the wall of our living room, relegating lesser sets to smaller spaces such as bedrooms, kitchens, and baths. We obsess over owning enough clothing so as not to wear the same outfit, silk tie, t-shirt, or "bling" twice in any given month. We can never have too much closet space, and those of us who own older homes wonder how our ancestors managed with so little. We drive Hummers and other gas guzzlers that roar out our arrival and intimidate lesser beings, whom we, literally, look down upon. Our resumes are weighted with the largess of our achievements, unrolled like a sacred scroll.

Yet, at the other end of the spectrum, we have taken to miniaturizing all manner of things, from cookies and crackers to human bodies—perhaps the most bizarre example being Michael Jackson's disappearing nose. Mini Coopers fly off the showroom floor. A popular retailer of women's apparel minimizes its sizes, and a traditional size four becomes a size zero. Who wouldn't want to wear a size zero in a culture that idolizes starving models' shrinking bodies? Cellular phones are so compact that a gaunt woman who barely squeezes into her jeans can still slip the phone into her back pocket. Perhaps the most extreme of all are those technologies such as wafer thin laptops, Black- and Blueberrys, and iPod nanos™, which represent the ultimate in infinities: the smallest size with the largest capacity. To have the infinitely large and the infinitely small is a sign of success, a symbol of our nearness to divinity, perhaps. In sum, the culture of one and infinity is a culture of desire, desire for the extremes that remain always just beyond our ability to grasp, experience, or fully comprehend.

Theologically, one and infinity cannot be denied or sidestepped. We speak of the one God known in three persons and of the infinite nature or being of God. But this language does not claim to speak of a numerical reality or to suggest a quantifiable mass; it points to a mystery associated with divine reality that cannot be fully explained and resists our attempts to come to closure. Thus, when the church focuses on the numbers' game, we are given a sign that our attention has turned away from the mystery of the living God to the calculable and calculating world of human desire, a world that pursues the extreme, the extraordinary, the extravagant. Football players who point their index fingers heavenward to give glory to God for their on-field scores differ only by a few inches of arm extension from the players indicating "we're number one." When did the church begin counting noses as a measure of God's favor? When did the largest churches become the epitome of Christ's way? When did we begin pointing our index fingers toward the sky and praising the numbers on high? The numbers' game is a poor substitute for radical relationship with God. It points to a world driven by and to excess, rather than being open and responsible toward God and others. In today's social and historical context, this compulsive pursuit of one and infinity takes the form of the three temptations now distorting our communities of faith: 1) consumerism (turning bread to stones); 2) individualism (throwing ourselves down from the pinnacle); and 3) imperialism (ruling all the kingdoms of the world). As we explore these features of contemporary society in the United States, our goal is to name and loosen the grip of the culture of one and infinity so that the church might begin to move beyond the situation of spiritual decline.

In rereading the temptation scene as a reflection of the contemporary captivity of the Christian church in the United States, we must first acknowledge the complexity of the factors of consumerism, individualism, and imperialism. Entire books have been written on each of these topics without arriving at conclusions about their nature, source, or impact. Moreover, it is virtually impossible to break open the convergence of factors to view one of them in isolation; as with most social, economic, political, and institutional structures of society, they form a tangled network with varied expressions in and shifting implications for our lives and world. In spite of these difficulties, if we hope to understand the church's decline, we need to examine each factor as a separate phenomenon with its own characteristics.

Our Passion for Consumption

We return now to Jesus of Nazareth fasting and praying in the wilderness. "The tempter came and said to him, 'If you are the Son of God, command these stones to become loaves of bread'" (Matt. 4:3). If you belong to the family of God, if you know God is with you and wants to bless you, then turn these stones into bread. Although it is easy for us to profess our willingness to choose God over the temptation of material objects, to say we put God before everything else in our lives, in truth we still want to turn stones into bread. We want to turn stones into the oil that fuels our cars idling in drive-through lanes at fast food restaurants and powers the "necessities" of our high-tech, climate-controlled, microwavable environments. We want to turn stones into polished diamonds, emeralds, pearls, and rubies set in gold, silver, and platinum. We want to turn stones into titanium-covered fighter jets pregnant with laser guided bombs. We want to turn stones into walls that protect our gated communities and into prisons to hold those who violate them. We want to turn stones into multi-million dollar sanctuaries with coffee shops and gymnasiums. We cry out for more stones, even as the earth wheezes and gasps, stripped bare of its beauty and integrity. We cry out for more stones, even as coal miners wheeze and gasp for a living wage and safe working conditions. Perhaps the epitome of this desire for turning stones into bread appeared some years ago in the form of "pet rocks," which were purchased by millions and shortly thereafter returned unceremoniously to the earth. Despite our protestations to the contrary, our actions suggest that we do, in fact, want to turn stones into bread as essential to our happiness.

Thus, we come to the first temptation that infects the church: our passion for consumption. To understand how and why today's churches succumb to this temptation to turn stones into bread, we need to recognize the logic of capitalism and how it has grown to unprecedented proportions through the media and advertising. Rodney Clapp, who has written extensively on Christianity and consumerism, argues that many "features of today's capitalism were either unimaginable or positively condemned throughout most of Christian history."[15] Drawing upon the work of Max Weber and Colin Campbell, Clapp explains that the Puritan work ethic was focused on production, not consumption, and certainly not enjoyment of consumption. The strong emotional sensibility of the Puritans was related to "intense introspection" and "a melancholy bearing, self-debasement, and fascination with one's own death [as] outward signs of inward godliness."[16] Romanticism subsequently "secularized" the Puritan emotionalism; in the wake of the Enlightenment and technological advances, intense emotional experiences themselves became a source of pleasure and self-fulfillment. Even so, before the industrial revolution took hold, our pleasures remained rather modest.

The rapid improvement in technologies in the late nineteenth and early twentieth centuries enabled the explosion of production and shifted capitalism from a production-based economy to one increasingly driven by consumption. It was now possible to produce goods far beyond what demand or need required. For example, "when James Buchanan Duke procured merely two Bonsack cigarette machines, he could immediately produce 240,000 cigarettes a day—more than the entire U.S. market smoked. Such production was the rule, not the exception."[17] The obvious answer to this dilemma, at least in the eyes of manufacturers, was to increase consumption by convincing people that they wanted or needed something to make their lives better or more fulfilling.

Into this milieu stepped the revivalists of the late nineteenth and early twentieth centuries, such as Charles Finney: "Revivalism encouraged rapturous feelings and a malleable self that is open time and again to the changes of conversion and reconversion. This was simply translated into a propensity toward 'conversion' to new products, a variety of brands, and fresh experiences."[18] Clapp notes that the origins of modern advertising can be traced to the patent-medicine peddled on the "fringes of revival meetings," which "drew directly on the before-and-after pattern of evangelical testimony," in which a product leads to "new life."[19] Under the revival tent, the cry may have been, "I once was lost but now am found," but just beyond the flap the cry became, "I once was sickly but now I'm strong" thanks to Doctor Hawker's tonic. Revivalism thus contributed to the growing link between consumerism and faith. In general, around the turn of the century, "a shift was made toward the cultivation of unbounded desire."[20]

Our consumer culture, as Vincent Miller argues, is not really about fulfillment, since objects inevitably disappoint us, but about the sheer and endless joy of desire itself, the endless prospect of becoming new. Moreover, the inculcation of such desire undermines our religious practices. To explain how desire functions, Miller describes two dynamics at work: "seduction," a term coined by sociologist Zygmunt Bauman, and what Miller calls "misdirection." Seduction operates by placing before us a "vast, undifferentiated horizon of *potential* fulfillments."[21] It creates an infinite number of objects for us to desire and expands our imagined needs. Infomercials convince us that our lives would be transformed by the mere purchase of a megachopper in our choice of colors. We are always in search of the next great Beanie Baby or software update. Pharmaceutical manufacturers urge us to ask our doctors if some medication is right for us, even though the advertisement might not mention what disease it is intended to ameliorate. Single serving coffee makers enable us to constantly recreate flavor combinations, and Hershey's Kisses come in limited release flavors. People camp out all night in front of their local discount store to be the first to own the latest Xbox game player, knowing that in a year or two it will be ousted by the next great dream thing. Today's televisions will soon be obsolete, and we worry that our old set will cease to receive our must-see programming. Will we wait too long to convert and find ourselves left behind? We are urged and prodded to begin desiring the new, the improved, the bigger, as that which is more life-giving. Is it any wonder that we shop for a church home that will give us a new, better, or more intense experience?

More troubling still is that the culture of desire begins early: before reaching school age, the average child in the United States will have spent as much time in front of a television set as he or she will later spend sitting in lectures over the course of four years of college. "The preponderance of programming and advertising in the U.S. delivers a continual message. . . . The only times that persons are presented as uniformly happy and ecstatically fulfilled are in commercials: purchasing, collecting or consuming products that resolve problems, deliver self-assurance, win friends."[22] Simply stated, the primary values and desires of people in the United States are being formed from an early age by the culture of consumption. How can one hour a week of church school compete with the average household's daily television viewing time of more than six hours? No wonder the "unchurched" and even those who consider themselves lifelong Christians approach their faith as they would a shopping trip to the mall: comparing options, test driving services, and seeking to get the most for their dollar. Is this not the "American way?" Clearly, we are socialized and formed by the media and advertising far more than we are by communities of faith, hope, and love. As Miller notes, "the insatiability of consumer desire arises . . . as a result of formation in the daily commerce of advanced capitalist economies."[23]

Combined with seduction is the dynamic of misdirection, which "evokes and sustains desire for commodities by associating them with unrelated human needs and desires."[24] Miller suggests that consumers in the United States "engage in consumption in order to fulfill the social needs for identity and belonging."[25] Who we understand ourselves to be is now a matter of conspicuous consumption and the acquisition of status products such as those found at the "coolhunting" web site and in the countless catalogues that show us what we never knew we needed and now cannot live without. Thus, combined with seduction, we are in a process of constantly recreating ourselves and desiring to become new and improved, a more "in" version of our previous self. The feminist liberationist becomes the corporate executive enamored with the "finer things" of the bourgeois class she once rejected, then later retires to a farm in the country to raise goats and make cheese. The muscle man becomes the actor who becomes the governor. The singer steeped in sexual innuendo and sensuous apparel becomes the writer of children's books. We become like onions: one transparent layer upon another with no deep sense of identity beyond the images and objects of our desire and the urgent need to become new and improved. More profoundly, whatever quality we seek, whether "competence, reliability, stability, [or] durability," when "we wear and use such an item, we are reassured that we too are competent and capable."[26]

Ultimately, it is not that we lose sight of God entirely; we continue to long for God, to experience restless hearts, as Augustine poetically expressed in his Confessions. But "unlike Augustine, we do not experience restlessness, *inquies*, as a discomfort, as a spur to change the way we live our lives [in order to better follow the way of Jesus Christ]. Rather, we consider it a source of pleasure."[27] Because our identity is not located in God, but in the sheer pleasure of desiring—whether objects or God—we become sidetracked. In the grip of consumer culture, the Christian journey is "in danger of being reduced to the part-time dabbling of the religious consumer" and "a shallow form of seekerism."[28] Our deepest longing can be filled by ecstatic experiences that become a substitute for the hard and risky journey toward God. The church that understands this consumption-driven desire can manipulate it to attract hordes of hungry seekers; the church that does not grasp its pervasiveness will find itself gradually reduced to a faithful remnant. And, of course, remnants are what we find on the "half-price" table.

While this temptation is far more complex and convicting than the brief synopsis offered here, we are able, nonetheless, to grapple with the profound effect of the consumer culture on Christian faith. The church is confronted with persons whose formation is, in many ways, antithetical to the gospel. To allow market research to define the contours of the church is to capitulate to the norms of culture, even if we brush a coat of "Jesus" over the surface. The scriptures compel us to care for the widow, the orphan, and the stranger among us and command us to feed the hungry and clothe the naked—something supply and demand principles do not understand. But we are so steeped in credit card debt and home equity loans and so poor in savings that, even though our society has grown increasingly affluent and the standard of living in the United States has grown, we can barely feed and clothe ourselves and have little left to share. So we come full circle in wanting to turn stones into bread so that we might have more to fill our endless desire.

Our Culture of Individualism

Again, we find ourselves in the wilderness with Jesus of Nazareth.

> Then the devil took him to the holy city and placed him on the pinnacle of the temple, saying to him, "If you are the Son of God, throw yourself down, for it is written,
>
> 'He will command his angels concerning you,'
> and 'On their hands they will bear you up,
> so that you will not dash your foot against a stone.'"
>
> (Matt. 4:5–6)

As we saw in our examination of consumerism, the *desire* for possessing things is more powerful than the actual enjoyment of the objects. This distorted yearning infects our society and churches, undermining the Spirit at work in the body of believers. Such desire is complicated and exacerbated by its locus: We do not desire justice or the reign of God or even to be conformed to the likeness of Christ, as much as we desire a better, improved, more meaningful self. The pattern of revivalism, in which once a year we desire an ecstatic experience that will remake us anew continues to function on a larger scale and compressed cycle. Now, rather than seeking God in the midst of the body of Christ, we are focused on the individual self, empowered by the Holy Spirit or possessing Jesus within, and the pursuit of its own limitless desires as the essence of the spiritual journey.

To be placed on the pinnacle represents success; it indicates that we have made it to the top. The pinnacle means nothing can touch us; not even our feet will be dashed against the stones we are turning into bread. We are insulated from the worries that plague the masses. We play "king of the hill" and dare others to knock us from the heights, assured that God is with us. For many contemporary Christians, reaching the pinnacle is the goal of the life of faith. God will lift us up if we only believe and pray and ask. Being "blessed" by God's "favor," we cannot be thrown down or come to any harm. Thus the devil shows us the pinnacle of the temple, reminds us that our own body is God's temple, and entices us: If you belong to God, then you have eternal life, and you need not worry for God will bless you, favor you, give you more than you ever imagined. Go ahead, be happy and do not fear, for God is with you.

Although we profess to be disciples who follow Jesus Christ, under the sway of the culture of individualism we succumb to a form of personal, individual "salvation" in which our actions belie our language of discipleship and misrepresent the gospel message. At times, when we profess Jesus as our personal Lord and Savior, we speak and think as if we are one with Christ, as if we possess God within our hearts—not unlike the many objects we desire. Rather than allowing the living God to "possess" us, we unwittingly turn God into another one of our possessions, a *deus ex machina* at our disposal. We want our best life now or to enlarge our territory or to be purpose-driven to discover what "I" am here for, rather than to discover who God in Christ in the Holy Spirit is in the midst of the world. Rick Warren urges us to "share our life's message" so that we can become "a world-class Christian," as if our journey is to earn a gold medal or loving cup to display on the mantel. We want to get to the pinnacle and to throw ourselves down, proving that we are chosen by God, destined for a good end, sure to be lifted up and blessed. We want certainty rather than the journey of faith.

Moreover, in seeking the pinnacle, we are prone to set ourselves apart from the messiness and difference of genuine community. If God and I are one, others become less crucial to my life as a follower of Christ and my understanding of that life. I do not really need anyone else to be whole—unless, of course, he or she fills my desire and needs. I choose my church, my Sunday school class, and the people with whom I associate in my congregation—all based on their ability to better satiate or deepen my desires, or at the very least, to make me feel comfortable. Perhaps deep down inside, we want to look into the face of the other and see a spark or reflection of ourselves. Today, we still want to be lifted to the pinnacle and thrown down to prove that we are God's chosen ones, to distinguish ourselves as more truly blessed, to fulfill our quest for self-actualization, as if life in God is a steady stream of higher highs and deeper pockets.

We want to be first. We play the lottery, promising God that, if our lucky numbers come up, we will tithe to the church before we buy our new BMW. We change lanes on the highway by speeding up and getting in front of other cars—our ICTHUS fish wagging its tail in their faces. Technology enables us to remain far more isolated and self-focused than at any previous time in history: we buy our groceries and use the self-checkout lane. We play computer games against disembodied opponents with user names. Our money is dispensed by a poker-faced ATM. Our calls to distant companies are answered by "voices," instructing us to choose numbers and blocking us from human contact. We fence in our homes, gate our communities, and post signs to warn that our dog will attack. We go church shopping to find a place, not where we can serve, but where our wishes can best be met. We skip Sunday worship because we want to do other things like sleep, walk in the woods, or go out to breakfast. No worries: Jesus is our personal Lord and Savior. We have a mobile, portable, pray-as-you-go God.

The second temptation that infects the church is this culture of individualism, which is a phenomenon gripping the larger society and originating in the lingering contours of modernity. Perhaps the study that first captured our awareness of our individualistic tendencies was *Habits of the Heart* by Robert Bellah and colleagues. *Habits of the Heart* argued that the language of individualism is the dominant discourse of life in the United States and shapes how we understand basic societal values like success, freedom, and justice. While the authors identified four strands of individualism within the culture, they also claimed that these approaches shared certain things "that are basic to American identity."[29] Modern individualism "stressed the dignity and autonomy of the individual" and often emphasized a "therapeutic ethos," in which the self is "the only or main form of reality."[30] This conception of the therapeutic self represents a significant shift: "[i]n the wake of the collapse of traditional frameworks of meaning, the modern self faced an increased demand to perform and be productive. This instrumentalized and commodified self was expressed in a shift in emphasis from character to 'personality.'. . . 'Growth,' 'becoming,' and 'self-realization' became ends in themselves, divorced from broader social or transcendent goals."[31] No wonder self-help books adorned with the language of God are so popular in our society.

Perhaps the epitome of modern individualism was the so-called "Sheilaism" identified in *Habits of the Heart* and based on interviews with Sheila Larson, who named her personal, experiential form of faith after herself. While most of us do not go so far as to name our faith in this manner, the emphasis on personal religious experience remains a significant force in American Christianity and infects both ends of the religious spectrum:

> Radically individualistic religion, particularly when it takes the form of a belief in cosmic selfhood, may seem to be in a different world from conservative or fundamentalist religion. Yet these are the two poles that organize much of American religious life. To the first, God is simply the

> self magnified; to the second, God confronts [us] from outside the universe. One seeks a self that is finally identical with the world; the other seeks an external God who will provide order in the world. Both value personal religious experience as the basis of their belief.[32]

Individualism focuses on the experiences and improvements of the solitary self—whether via autonomous freedom or heteronomous control—rather than on communal and social values and relationships as primary to life in God. Faith is about creating my best life now and experiencing emotional religious "highs."

In the years since *Habits of the Heart* first appeared, the study has been criticized for its tendency toward narrowness and overgeneralization.[33] Yet its basic contention remains the subject of discussion: As a society, the United States is filled with persons who are predominantly, though not exclusively, self-concerned and self-motivated. As Robert Putnam pointed out, some fifteen years after Bellah's study, social capital and participation in various social organizations, including religious communities, continue to decline across U.S. society.[34] Although Christian faith is always about life together in a community where Christ is the face we present to the world, increasingly we want to put on our own best face and take it out into the world.

This analysis of individualism in the United States is deepened and attenuated by the historical framework of Charles Taylor, who traces the rise of the modern "self" from Plato through Derrida and Foucault and identifies the gradual "dissipation of our sense of the cosmos as a meaningful order."[35] The self is constructed in relationship to some notion of the good, and a self cannot exist apart from reference to other selves—or, if we refer back to the problem of consumerism, it cannot exist apart from reference to other idealized selves. In today's culture, the good is consumption and other selves are the multitude of images that stir up our desire to be remade as a better self. Moreover, our identity has a narrative content, in which we construct a story of our self: "In order to have a sense of who we are, we have to have a notion of how we have become, and of where we are going."[36] We are in a constant process of desiring improvement and seeking greater self-fulfillment and of characterizing ourselves as either "better" than we used to be or "less" successful, affluent, attractive, thin, loved. In the modern period—due to the enlightened loss of the cosmos and the rise of our desire-filled lives—the self becomes constituted by and focused on inwardness."[37] Inwardness points toward the ultimacy of the feelings and thoughts that lie deep within us. How I feel and what I think become my guiding forces—never mind that the media and advertising hold me captive. This inwardness, this emphasis on individual thoughts and feelings, this centrality of the inner heart and mind leads to the "disenchantment" of the world. Ideas no longer exist "out there" in the cosmos, but are now found "in here," within the individual, autonomous human being. The question, "What's in it for me?" becomes central to our life's journey.

This "reflexive project of the self, which consists in the sustaining of coherent, yet continuously revised, biographical narratives, takes place in the context of multiple choice."[38] Because we live in a "post-traditional" society, we are compelled to answer the question, "'How shall I live?' . . . in day-to-day decisions about how to behave, what to wear and what to eat—and many other things . . ." and all such answers are interpreted and reinterpreted as constitutive of our self-identity.[39] In traditional societies, life transitions or moments when the self is reconceived often entail rites of passage in which older generations help to make sense of the new identity, something that communities of faith have typically understood and participated in. Today, however, we must choose our own lifestyle and continually interpret ourselves in the face of an unstable and fragmented world, which is far more present to us than ever before. In a society whose mantra is "out with the old," we find little wisdom in the aged and are bored with anything "traditional." We are compelled to search within ourselves, to "find" ourselves, to make meaning out of the events and decisions of our lives, and to become a healthy and whole self in and through this interior process—all driven by our media and image filled milieu. We choose the rituals, images, and experiences that we find meaningful. Traditional symbols and rites such as the sacraments of the church gradually lose their meaning and lack the ability to convey a sense of who we are as people of God and who we are called to become. Some churches follow the "out with the old" mentality, viewing Christian symbols as an old wardrobe in need of updating, as embarrassingly old-fashioned. Others doggedly administer the sacraments, but few seem to be deeply moved and formed by them. Many people simply choose whatever symbols or rituals speak to them as individuals and discard the rest. No matter the tradition from which they arise or the symbolism once intended, images are free for the taking and appropriating.

This inwardness and lack of an external public or communal order of meaning represents a radical shift in what it means to be a self. In the earliest Christian communities up through the Reformation and into the origins of Christianity in the United States, there existed a "publicly available background" of beliefs in God (theology) and the cosmos (metaphysics) that simply does not exist in the modern era and today's postmodern society.[40] For example, Martin Luther's "intense anguish and distress before his liberating moment of insight about salvation through faith, his sense of inescapable condemnation . . . was not a crisis of meaning. This term would have made no sense to Luther. . . . The 'meaning' of life was all too unquestionable for this Augustinian monk, as it was for his whole age."[41] Luther lived in a world that was mediated to him by traditions and traditional authorities; our world is constructed from the inside out and we must "make sense" of our lives. Is it any wonder that Jesus now lives "in" me? Of course, we should acknowledge that Luther's world view was hierarchical, patriarchal, and exclusionary: liberationists and feminists have opened our eyes to the problems associated with traditional systems of authority and urged us to develop new forms of community that resemble early Christian communities in their concern for inclusion and social and economic egalitarianism.

But in reality, our contemporary ideals of autonomy, freedom, and individual rights also often exclude and marginalize in practice. Those who seek self-fulfillment are likely to understand themselves as the center of their own moral universe. Not only can this lead to judgmental attitudes that are relativistic in nature, but it also distorts self-love. Sometimes the self is elevated to the primary position in a narrative of Augustinian pride. Sometimes the self is wholly given away for others as in the traditional role of the nurturing caregiver whose self exists only in the doing for others. Either way, it is a self that has lost touch with the reality of God. The self enamored with uplifting, exalting experiences of presence and self-transformation loses touch with the transcendent God who "exists" apart from our journey of self-fulfillment and self-improvement. God does not respond to our every whim and desire for personal feeling and development and does not "exist" simply to bless me with more, better, and bigger. At the same time, the self enamored with others has lost touch with the reality of the immanent God. God is with us and seeks to be in radical relationship with us; God loves and affirms who we are created to be and knows us by name. God wants us to be fully human, not utterly selfless. The emphasis on the self and its role in identity formation means we are in a constant process of self-examination. Our supposed goal is to become the best self we can be in each given moment, in light of all possibilities before us, whether receiving more or giving more.

The options placed before us seem endless, and we are deluded into believing that all people have the same infinite possibilities for constructing the perfect self; they need only make the right personal decisions, lift themselves up by their bootstraps, learn proper family values, watch Dr. Phil or the 700 Club regularly. Thus, the narrative of the self argues that the seventeen-year-old, unwed, unemployed, inner city mother has created this situation on her own. The prisons filled with African American men could be emptied if these men would only choose to be different selves. The problems of poverty and violence in places such as Guatemala, Sudan, and Afghanistan are, at heart, a function of choices that undermine their construction of the perfect self. It seems that they do not even desire to be on this inward journey of free, autonomous, or heteronomous self-discovery and self-fulfillment; if they did, they could "fix" their lives.

The notion that each individual can receive the same blessings from God, if they only pray in the right way or make better moral decisions, is the language of Individualism. The "I" that stands apart from others and points fingers in judgment is an individual self that rejects radical relationship with God and others. It is a self that ignores the ways in which social and cultural institutions undermine the dignity and flourishing of human life. This "I" is prone to judgment, not love. Christian community is a reality in which the radically relational self, the Christ character, is formed within the tension and fluidity of giving and receiving life. It recognizes that we are complicit in the "failures" of others and they are participants in our own "successes," as we allow social-political-economic structures of our society to undermine the possibilities for life of the many while prescribing individual norms of "morality." The unwed teenage mother is labeled as morally corrupt while our corporate retirement plans buy stocks in software manufactures and recording dynasties that sell sex and violence to teenagers. We refuse to raise the minimum wage, while CEOs of failing companies receive multimillion dollar bonuses. Minutemen take the law into their hands to prevent persons from crossing the border while U.S. companies build factories in impoverished nations where labor laws are few and far between. Churches that cater to the preeminence of the individual are likely not only to feed the desire for self-fulfillment, but also to condemn those who do not agree with their experience of Christian faith. They feel compelled to pursue public policies that can force others to conform to their notion of the perfected self. If we can only get Roe versus Wade reversed, our country will be "Christian," no matter that the rich will still be able to obtain abortions, as was true in the past. If we can only prohibit all gay marriages or commitment services, we will uphold family values—as if all heterosexual marriages are models of love and caring and we can legislate right relationship. Unfortunately, it has never been possible to legislate or require faith in God and adherence to Christian values by means of the law. Prohibition is but one glaring example of the misguided desire to force others to follow the supposed way of Christ. Indeed, if we could legislate right behavior and right relationship, there would be no need for God in Christ in the Holy Spirit and the way that leads to life abundant.

The gospel is a life-centered discourse, and it functions to confront us with the chains we place on the lives of others—or on ourselves—demanding not that "they" change, but seeing how we too must change. To force a certain morality and belief as the only allowable form of the self is to serve as judge over others and to limit the image of God to a narrow and quite human conception. We lose sight of our inability to know with perfect wisdom; we succumb to the serpent's lie and believe that we are "God-like" by virtue of faith. But the Christian person living by faith, hope, and love in God chooses a different path to wholeness, sometimes following the gentle, patient way of love and sometimes the risky path of the prophet as these routes lead toward the flourishing of humanity and the whole of creation. Both patient love and prophetic boldness inevitably entail some discomfort, and we should not expect to grow increasingly comfortable, especially if we are following the way of God in Christ in the Holy Spirit proclaimed in the scriptures. The way of Jesus always keeps us a little off balance, reminding us never to confuse our own conclusions and presumptions with the fullness of God's will. The way of Jesus continues to hold a mirror before us in which we see dimly.

In sum, the pinnacle cannot be our goal, for under the logic of the pinnacle, the point is self-serving, a hierarchical impulse toward being closer to God and more beloved, often at the expense or disregard of others or our own deepest humanity. But God does not value a small part of creation above the rest; God upholds and loves the whole of creation. To choose the pinnacle is to close ourselves to God, others, the whole of creation, and ultimately, to the fullness of our humanity.

Our Desire to Rule the World

We return now to Jesus of Nazareth in the wilderness and face the third temptation:

> Again, the devil took him to a very high mountain and showed him all the kingdoms of the world and their splendor; and he said to him, "All these I will give you, if you will fall down and worship me." (Matt. 4:8–9)

Having examined the problems of consumerism and individualism, we come to the third cultural factor infecting U.S. churches: imperialism. For many Christians, raising political and economic questions is inappropriate in a book about Christian faith and the church; Christian faith is set apart from such "worldly" concerns. Yet reading the Bible and engaging in theological reflection necessarily entail political consequences. Justo González suggests that when we seek to make Christianity "apolitical," we in fact are supporting the political agenda of the powerful and privileged. He writes,

> What is usually meant by "mixing politics and religion" is very selective, depending on what kind of politics is actually mixed with religion. To pray at the U.S. Congress, to preach in the White House, or to "give a blessing" at a stockholders' meeting is not political and therefore acceptable. But to speak at a farm workers' rally, to bless their efforts to organize, or to criticize the Immigration Service is political. To attend a prayer breakfast with the governor of Puerto Rico is not political. To protest the presence of the Navy in Vieques is political. If one looks at the clear contradictions in such views, it is clear that the "apolitical" understanding of Christianity is very political indeed and is intended to support the agenda of the status quo.[42]

In subtle and not so subtle ways, Christians in the United States demonstrate a strong desire to have all the kingdoms of the world under U.S. control, and we are unabashedly political. Nonbelievers and Christians alike chant, "USA, USA" and "We're number one!" In many venues, Christians are indistinguishable from the crowds, other than waving our John 3:16 placards. We support foreign policies enabling the United States to act unilaterally with military force whenever our "interests" are threatened. We believe it is our God-given duty to protect the world, and our military spending in 2003 and 2004 exceeded the spending by the rest of the world combined.[43] We condemn human rights abuses in other lands, but operate secret prisons and engage in torture in the name of democracy and freedom.

Christians are called to be cocaretakers of the earth, yet because we are "blessed" to have such a high-tech, mobile, affluent society, we greedily gobble up the earth's resources. The use of energy in the United States has grown by more than 30 percent over the last quarter century.[44] We are home to some 5 percent of the world's population, but responsible for 25 percent of global emissions of carbon dioxide; nine times the world average of per capita annual gasoline consumption; more than one-third of the total transportation usage worldwide; and an "ecological footprint" four times greater than the global average.[45] We model to others conspicuous consumption as the basis of the good life.

It is said that it is more blessed to give than to receive, yet we continue to create and sustain economic policies that enable the rich to become richer and the poor to become poorer. In the United States, the top 1 percent of income earners now account for "seventeen percent of gross income, a level last seen in the 1920s."[46] Globally, it is estimated that more than "one billion people still live below the extreme poverty line of one dollar per day, and 20,000 die from poverty each day. Overall global wealth has grown but is less and less evenly distributed within countries, within regions and in the world as a whole."[47] The world's hunger appears on our television and computer screens almost daily, while we eat our freshly delivered double topping pizza and throw away the crust. But what can we do? After all, our parents once chastised us to clean our plates, pointing to the hungry children in China, but we knew sending the leftovers to Beijing would be impossible. Even so, the United Nations maintains that, "there is more than enough food in the world for all its inhabitants, and low-cost food supplies are produced in quantities sufficient to meet the needs of the growing global population. If food was distributed equitably around the world, enough would be available for everyone to consume an average of 2,760 calories a day. . . . In spite of these facts and possibilities, appalling nutritional inequalities persist throughout the world."[48] The inequalities are exacerbated by the social and cultural mores under which women, children, and the elderly receive proportionately less food than adult men in most of the world.[49] One-half of the ten million children who die every year in the developing world die of malnutrition, while obesity is a growing problem in the developed countries.[50] Some estimates suggest that as many as one in five in the United States are now considered obese. Clearly, bigger is not always better.

Those who believe that there is a clear separation of church and state in the United States and that the kingdom of God and the kingdom of humanity are sharply distinguished are turning a blind eye to the facts. Our churches celebrate the fourth of July, honor the military on Veteran's Day, and talk of the United States as God's chosen nation. Our coinage proclaims, "In God we trust," rather than "Give unto Caesar what is Caesar's." A large urban congregation processes with the U.S. flag on Sunday mornings and sings a chorus of "America" after the doxology, even when the visiting preacher is British. Megachurches spend tens of millions of dollars on "auditoriums" that serve the middle and upper classes with a healthy dose of patriotism and the prosperity gospel. The rhetoric of the United States is that of a "Christian" nation when it serves our purposes; the rhetoric points to the separation of church and state when it does not. We do not claim that our churches are national churches, even though they wrap themselves in the language and cultural trappings of the nation. In reality, our slippery church and nation rhetoric has often been used to mask the language of empire and imperial desires, which swallow up the gospel and lead the churches to become complicit. In a sense, the logic of individualism is projected onto the collective identity of the nation, and the United States becomes an affluent, Christian Self seeking continual improvement, increasing wealth, greater power, more blessed successes. We want to reign over all other nations of the world in the name of God, to prove that our nation rules the earth.

Since at least the latter part of the nineteenth century, the United States has been on a path toward becoming an empire, and we have been enamored with the notion that our destiny is tied to God's favor. From the fledgling nation's continental expansion—at the expense of the native peoples—to the present day, the notion and, eventually, the language of manifest destiny shaped the collective consciousness of the country. We believe ourselves to be set apart by God; indeed, the myth or symbol of "America" can be viewed as the Pilgrim's homecoming, the arrival at the promised land flowing with milk and honey—at least for the free, white male.[51]

Of course, up until World War II, the United States often pursued isolationist policies and avoided the route of direct rule, especially since colonialism had begun to unravel around the world. But with the fall of Imperial Japan and Hitler's Germany, the United States moved into a new position as one of two superpowers in the world, engaged in a struggle for supremacy. Throughout the Cold War era, the world became divided into East and West, in a delicate balancing act of global power that the United States often described in terms of the good, virtuous, and moral Christian nation nobly holding at bay the godless forces with imperial designs. At times we supported dictatorial regimes in other countries, hoping they would serve our interests no matter how brutal or corrupt they might be toward their own people. But with the virtual end of communism in the 1990s and the subsequent disintegration of the Soviet Union, the United States declared victory and became the sole global power and the center of a unipolar world. This new position of dominance was based on economic and cultural factors as much as military and political ones.[52] Capitalism, after all, had won out; it had proven its superiority. As a result, we increasingly exported the "American way of life" as the spoils of war: McDonalds sprouted up in every major city of the world and Disneyland magically appeared in France, not to mention that Levis now label waists across the face of the earth.

Without naming its rise as an empire, the United States began to function as one: "on a global scale the United States has and seeks to exercise sufficient power over the political and economic priorities of other nations and the international system as a whole so as to serve the interests of powerful sectors within the United States."[53] Today, the country's power holders openly acknowledge this desire to rule over all the nations of the world. Notably, in 2004, a senior advisor to the president declared that, "We're an empire now, and when we act, we create our own reality."[54] We now find ourselves in a position to rule over all the kingdoms of the world and their splendor.

When the United States seeks a position of dominance over other nations and peoples, and Christians support or contribute to this desire to rule over others, we succumb to the third temptation faced by Jesus of Nazareth, the desire to rule over the entire world. The relationship between Christianity and empire takes many forms: the rhetoric of the United States as God's nation or the chosen people; the support of churches for preemptive military actions; the belief that U.S. power is an "instrument of God's justice or God's vengeance"; even the blurring of lines between faith and patriotism.[55] Here the logic is that we will bring the reign of God by force if we must, and then we will rule in God's name. Especially problematic is this idea of "American exceptionalism," in which the United States is believed to possess the sole right, "whether by divine sanction or moral obligation, to bring civilization, or democracy, or liberty to the rest of the world, by violence if necessary."[56] We fall prey to the rhetoric of the Christian nation standing strong against the evil axis, destined by God to be the protector of freedom and democracy, by any means necessary. But "[d]ivine ordination is a very dangerous idea, especially when combined with military power. . . . With God's approval, you need no human standard of morality."[57] Thus, we become self-justifying, taking judgment into our own hands, taking God's name in vain.

Where do Christians get the idea that identifying with national boundaries is God's will? How do people of faith support the claim that the United States is "chosen" by God for a "special" role in the world? We turn, of course, to the Bible for justification, and there we read our desire for power into the text. Yet, when we let the scriptures speak to us, we cannot help but notice that the message of Jesus and the earliest Christians confronted earthly powers and opposed the Roman Empire and its imperial desires. Richard Horsley argues that central to the gospel message of the historical Jesus is precisely an opposition to imperial powers: "the dominant plot of the Gospel has two complementary aspects, the renewal of Israel and the condemnation of the rulers."[58] He further notes that in the Gospel of Mark, for example, the central theme of the kingdom of God weaves together the two basic pieces of the overall gospel message: "The counterpart of the renewal of Israel as the realization of the Kingdom of God is the judgment of the oppressive rulers of Israel by the kingly rule of God."[59] In other words, the reign of God is not to be confused with earthly powers that are destined to be judged for the ways in which they have wielded power over other peoples. If the United States believes itself to be above the judgment of God or identifies itself with God's will for humanity, we are not attending carefully to the message of the scriptural witnesses.

Moreover, we tend to think that "Jesus was preaching a spiritual kingdom, while Caesar headed the temporal kingdom—but we now recognize that as a later self-protective and accommodationist Christian projection."[60] For example, we tend to read Jesus' answer to the question of paying tribute to Caesar as meaning we should separate religion from politics and economics. But in the original context of ancient Israel and the Mosaic covenantal law under which paying tribute to Rome was not lawful, Jesus was actually saying, "If God is the exclusive Lord and Master, if the people of Israel live under the exclusive kingship of God, then all things belong to God, the implications for Caesar being fairly obvious. Jesus is clearly and simply reasserting the Israelite principle that Caesar, or any other imperial ruler, has no claim on the Israelite people."[61] When we peel back the lens of our cultural perspective, again and again we find that the message of Jesus stands against imperial designs. Above all, Horsley argues, "Jesus acted to heal the effects of empire and to summon people to rebuild their community life. In the conviction that the kingdom of God was at hand, he pressed a program of social revolution to reestablish just egalitarian and mutually supportive social-economic relations."[62] The message of Jesus is one of community, not self; of mutuality, not superiority; of the reign of God, not the rule of nations or empires.

As difficult as it is to admit, in many ways the United States today is more akin to the Roman Empire than the faithful, often beleaguered Christians of the ancient world. We want to secure our collective place on the pinnacle of the world while we turn our stones into bread. We seek to solidify our superior status. We act as if the living God has said to us: "All these I will give you, if you will fall down and worship me" (Matt. 4:8–9). We forget that Jesus rejected this offer in the wilderness and chose to worship and serve God only. Life in God is not about being lifted up above other peoples and nations, but putting down our swords, sharing our wealth, feeding the hungry, clothing the naked. And so we find ourselves again in the wilderness reaching out for the mantel of power, conceding our relationship to God for the sake of ruling all the nations of the world—all the while convincing ourselves that ruling others is God's will for the United States. But just as it is impossible to serve both God and mammon, it is also impossible to serve both God and the power of the world.

RECONNECTING WITH THE SPIRIT OF LIFE

We should not deceive ourselves into believing that the problem with the church in the United States can be solved, as many advocates of evangelism suggest, either by updating and contemporizing life together or by returning to more traditional structures of catechesis and order. We cannot simply develop a marketing plan or a series of Bible studies to fix what ails us. On the one hand, those churches that cater to what the "market" demands fall prey to the temptations and desires that are prevalent in today's society. Megachurches cancel worship services when they fall on Christmas. Sermons are replaced by dramatic performances and jazz bands. The passion narrative is depicted in bloody and violent detail on the silver screen, while we munch on our tub of hot buttered popcorn and weep over what Jesus did for us. Sanctuaries include coffee bars in the back for those who need a place to feel more comfortable with God. Any talk of sin becomes a sin; people want self-improvement and feel-good stories. While these churches are able to tally the numbers and proclaim great success in meeting the needs of the masses, the deeper meaning of life in God must be set aside in large measure.

On the other hand, those churches that steadfastly stick to the tried-and-true of the fifth, sixteenth, or nineteenth centuries find their numbers dwindling and their congregations graying. Newcomers experience the church as a weekly chore to be scratched off the to-do list, the children dragged to Sunday school kicking and screaming. We sing "How Great Thou Art" in a whisper; turn to glare at anyone who dares to say, "Amen," during the sermon; watch the clock strike noon; and hurry off to shed our Sunday best in favor of greater pleasures and the weeklong pursuit of our desires. These churches linger like a bookmark: We have read several chapters, but it has not captured our imagination and we cannot quite seem to finish it. Unmoved, it gathers dust.

We can see that the problem with the Christian church in the United States lies deeper than the structures and methods of our institutional churches. The problem is not a matter of numbers or of programming. At heart, it is spiritual in nature. It is about relationship with God in Christ in the Holy Spirit and, in and through God, with the whole of creation. Ronald Rolheiser begins his book *The Holy Longing* by suggesting that to be human is to be filled with desire: "there is within us a fundamental dis-ease, an unquenchable fire that renders us incapable, in this life, of ever coming to full peace. This desire lies at the deep center of our lives. . . . We are driven persons, forever obsessed, congenitally dis-eased. . . ."[63] He goes on to say that we have a fire that burns within us, and "[w]hat we do with that fire, how we channel it, is our spirituality."[64] Our desire will shape our actions in and attitudes toward the world. If our central desire is for material goods, for self-actualization, or for worldly power, then our spirituality will not be turned toward God, no matter how much we may clothe our desire in the language of faith. While, today, "spirituality" can be found on every street corner and in businesses great and small, the spirit of the churches has become virtually indistinguishable from the spirits driven by desires other than the desire for God in Christ in the Holy Spirit.

This misplaced desire should not be understood as the absence of God from the churches or the United States. It is not, as some conservative commentators have cautioned, that God has removed God's "protective shield," as if God positions a divine Strategic Defense Initiative over the most favored nation at any given time. As Christians, we believe in the immanence of the God who has said, "I am with you till the end of the age." God's grace is always reaching out to humanity. But we are given the gift of free will in order to respond or to ignore that graceful initiative. Thus, the diminishment of the Spirit in the church is not a matter of God's withdrawal, but of our unwillingness to be formed by the depth of God's restorative power. Such a transformation does not make us into the idealized image of the surrounding culture, but forms us into the Christ character, the reality of God taking shape within us and through us in the world, a reality that runs counter to consumerism, individualism, and imperialism. We cannot seek and serve all gods.

The way we still the Spirit within our churches and close off its transformative power is both subtle and startling. In two simple steps we are able to justify the way of the world while claiming the fierce following of Christ. We enable ourselves to act *as if* we are living a God-centered, Jesus-led, Spirit-filled life. First, we depoliticize Jesus. This move enables us to "separate" the spiritual from the material aspects of our lives. We claim that Jesus of Nazareth had no interest in political, social, or economic affairs, but only spiritual matters. Jesus came to save us from our sins and avoided political issues. He came to give us spiritual renewal, not to challenge governments or the distribution of wealth. Yet, in the gospels, Jesus spoke and acted in ways that opposed and criticized the Roman Empire. His concern with feeding the hungry and clothing the naked has clear economic implications: redistributing goods from the haves to the have-nots. Moreover, in virtually every gospel story about Jesus, he confronted social mores such as the marginalization of women and children or the dehumanization of others based upon characteristics such as their occupation (for example, tax collectors) or ethnicity (for example, Samaritans). When we read the gospels, it becomes clear that we cannot separate these more "earthly" things from the spiritual realm, since the whole of creation belongs to God. When we separate the material from the spiritual, we cut off the Spirit of God in our midst.

Remarkably, once we have managed to separate the realm of religion from politics and economics through depoliticizing Jesus, we can then reclaim material aspects as part of our "spiritual" lives. In what is actually an incredible logical leap, the idea of being "in Christ," "born again," a follower of Jesus, or however we term our faith commitment, leads us to claim a new spiritual reality in which we belong not to the world, but to God. Once we are free from the earthly entanglements of the sinner—or put another way, "saved"—we can now claim all earthly treasures in the name of God, so long as we can forward certain strict "moral" claims about bodily behaviors, often related to sexuality. Amassing unlimited wealth is a sign of God's favor, so long as we write an occasional check for the needy. Never mind the story of Lazarus and the rich man. Certain Christians who hold rigid pro-life stances intended to save the life of every unborn child will applaud a sentence of death when the same child grows up and commits a heinous crime. Never mind that the Ten Commandments insist, "Thou shalt not kill," without adding, "unless of course the person is really bad and very frightening and lives in Texas." Claiming to be of the "Spirit," we find ourselves able to make claims that are highly political yet couched in the language of morality, which is deemed within the church's purview. Those churches who avoid such moral statements and simply exist to "worship God" are, themselves, making a political statement. As González notes, they are indicating that the status quo favors them and they would rather not see political, economic, and social systems change.

Yet the One we worship and profess to emulate turned existing political, economic, and social systems on their heads. In a religious tradition where the Messiah was expected to be a military genius and skilled warrior, Jesus of Nazareth refused to pick up a sword and claimed that peace is more powerful than brute force. In a society where wealth was valued, Jesus of Nazareth counseled followers to travel lightly through life rather than encumbered with the spoils of "success," and he cautioned them not to lay up treasures on earth lest they lose their treasure in heaven. In a political and cultural system in which women and children were the property of men, Jesus welcomed them as equals, offering them hospitality, friendship, healing, the fullness of life. In word and deed, Jesus of Nazareth challenged the existing powers and systems, offering the possibility of transformation from brokenness to the wholeness of radical relationality for all of creation. In Jesus, life in the Spirit meant a radically reoriented existence, a qualitatively different existence. When following Jesus is equated with a quantitative increase in worldly wealth, individual success, and national power, we have turned the gospel on its head and recreated life in God in our own images and desires.

In an ultimate sense, there is only one God who is the essence of infinity and whom we Christians name as God in Christ in the Holy Spirit. In the Triune God there is but one church whose holiness, justice, and saving grace exist only by means of our willingness to enter into relationship with God, to be formed into the Christ character, and to find ourselves led into the wilderness by the Holy Spirit to choose God over the world's wonders. We must begin this journey by acknowledging that we have desired many things above or before we have desired the living God and have used God's name to justify our own ways. While calling upon the Spirit we have chased after other spirits. Until we are able to turn back to the one, infinite God, the church in the United States will not find its way out of the wilderness in which it now exists. Until we are able to reorient our lives, no method or program of evangelism will fix what ails us. The answer does not begin with constructing new models for church growth—whether designed to remake the church in a more entertaining and media-filled image or to reclaim some idealized past version of the church. The answer begins with reorienting our lives so that God can form in us a new identity that differs from the desires that now infect our culture and churches.

As we turn to chapter 2, our journey toward opening ourselves to this new identity rooted in the practice of Godbearing will first examine the traditional practice and understanding of evangelism. We can then demonstrate that we need new language and images to help us re-turn (turn again) to God in Christ in the Holy Spirit. Indeed, the contemporary emphasis on "evangelism," in which pastors are required to be "evangelists" and churches are urged to become "evangelizing congregations," is actually counterproductive, in many ways, to the renewal of the Christian faith in North America. If we can understand why evangelism as conceived and practiced today isn't the answer, then we can move toward a more authentic embodiment of the gospel of Jesus Christ, reconceived as Godbearing.

two WHY "EVANGELISM" ISN'T THE ANSWER

As we have seen in chapter 1, we live in a time of extremes and numbers, technology and innovation. Our lives are framed by the expectation and illusion of quick fixes, easy answers, and constant control. Because we live in an age that seeks solutions to whatever ails us, we are drawn toward the possibilities found in technology, science, psychotherapy, and pharmaceuticals. Whatever the problem might be, an answer is just a patent, research grant, or infomercial away. With the right combination of machines, materials, and money, our advanced society will find the way around any impasse. At the same time, we embrace the notion that we are largely in control of our lives: our heating, air-conditioning, electricity, on-the-go phones and instant messaging, overnight express mail, and alarm systems are readily adjusted with the flick of a wrist. We configure our environment to suit our every whim and imagined need. It lulls us into a false sense of security and gives the impression that we are in control—at least until a powerful storm or battery failure disrupts our confident and carefree existence.

So it is hardly surprising that we are lulled into believing that our faith, too, belongs to the age of solutions and control. When the church is in decline, we can reinvigorate it if we pay attention to the right things. If we spend enough money on research and collect enough data, if we change the batteries and update our sanctuary systems, if we earn an MBA and send out ten thousand high resolution flyers, we can bring the church back to life or grow it to unprecedented levels. All we need to do is train our churches and their leaders in evangelism. We dream of a steady stream of seekers, who fit our demographic research profiles, rushing through the doors, convinced that our media message, upbeat music, symbol-free signature, casual wear, and cornucopia of growth groups will turn the ship around. Or if we are bursting at the seams, we have the evidence, the sheer numerical data, to prove God's presence among us and to urge others to follow our way. Although we will vigorously defend our claim that the Christian faith is "countercultural," our attitude toward renewing the church arises largely out of cultural assumptions and expectations, even though scriptural proof texts and the language of faith may be offered.

Indeed, there is something desperately human about the emphasis on evangelism in contemporary churches. At times, we seem more attuned to the numbers' game than we do to the reality of God with and among us. We focus on counting noses, assuming that more is better. We ask ourselves what we must add to attract new members. We are desperate to show signs of numerical growth as a measure of our ecclesial "success." Yet, beneath all this lies an emphasis on human production and on worldly standards of achievement. Perhaps we should pause long enough to ask if God calls us to undertake "evangelism" as the basis of our life together and, if so, what that really means. What is evangelism and where did it come from anyway? Some would have us think that it was the very heart of the message of Jesus Christ and central to the proclamation of the earliest Christians.

To answer the question of evangelism's origins and evolution, we begin by wading into the messiness of the word in order to recognize, first, that evangelism is not synonymous with evangelicalism, and second, that the meaning of sharing the good news is richer, deeper, and wider than most advocates of evangelism suggest. If we seek to renew the church, we need to explore the unfortunate conflation of evangelism and evangelicalism, the biblical roots of evangelism, and the historical emergence of the word and its connotations. Once we recognize the inadequacy of the word and practice of contemporary evangelism, we can then discover a new language, the language of Godbearing, as a better way to convey the depths of the gospel in the world.

We might say that, in today's usage, the word "evangelism" is "muddy." It lacks clarity in its definition and the practices it engenders. Such confusion leads many persons in the United States either to reject the topic of evangelism outright or to proclaim it as the savior of the church's decline. Moreover, the dominant voices in evangelism tend to offer a narrow evangelical theological perspective that discounts the historical and cultural realities surrounding Christianity in North America, preferring to view Christian faith as a closed system or internal grammar that is strictly and unabashedly set apart from the world—something that is misleading and even a dangerous lure for followers of Christ. Meanwhile, proponents of the megachurch model aimed at attracting "seekers" by marketing the church according to consumer preferences tend, at times, to use the gospel as decoration or slick promotional material. Many mainline denominations take up the evangelism banner as necessary to growing the church and tallying more satisfying numbers. Evangelism becomes like clay, shaped and recast to suit our perceived needs and desires, rather than having an inherent form and precise definition.

Moreover, we tend to view evangelism as a more "conservative" practice of the church. Our images are of televangelists with slick hair, well-thumbed Bible in hand, and of polite door-to-door canvassers with doomsday magazines. These purveyors of Christian faith continue to convey an either/or message of following Jesus or traveling a sure course to hell. In response to such images, many mainline congregations believe evangelism and its message conflicts with the desire for openness and interreligious dialogue, our sensitivity to difference, and our call to love all persons. At this end of the theological spectrum, we are uncomfortable with "traditional" notions of Gospel-sharing and conversion. Requiring such churches and pastors to engage in "evangelism" bears little fruit.

So we find ourselves on the horns of a dilemma: evangelism is the answer and it is not the answer. Evangelism will build strong churches in twelve ways or six easy steps; evangelism is the path of false prophets and judgmentalism. We vacillate between wanting to open our lives to the Spirit of God and being put off by those images and practices of evangelism that seem utterly human and manipulative. We no longer have a clear idea of what evangelism is, where it came from, who invented it, or if it is even a biblical concept. So, in order to move beyond this dilemma, we want to consider what evangelism is and what it is not.

EVANGELISM IS NOT EVANGELICALISM

While working on this book, a good friend asked me what I was writing about. When I responded, "evangelism," she visibly recoiled and said, "Oh, I don't see you as one of *those* Christians. You're much too progressive." Of course, one of the immediate difficulties with the topic of evangelism is its relationship—supposed or real—to evangelicalism and the baggage the term conveys, whether rightly or not. The words sound alike, as their common etymology is from the Greek meaning "good news," and evangelism has typically been a central activity or concern of evangelicals. It would seem that evangelism belongs to a narrow but vocal segment of the Christian church, and we shudder at the political pronouncements of evangelicals in the United States. But do we really know what an evangelical is or does or believes? And once we do, does such a position demonstrate and embody what evangelism calls us to be and to do?

Defining Evangelicalism

Mark Noll, a Christian historian and self-identified evangelical, has written extensively on the meaning and development of evangelicalism in the U.S. context. As is true of most religious movements, any attempt to neatly categorize persons as evangelical is elusive, since the term can be used in several different senses. Noll identifies at least four separate strands of meaning associated with evangelicalism. First, he suggests that the word has often been used "to describe God's redemption of sinners by the work of Christ."[1] Depending on how we interpret this statement, it could apply to virtually all Christians.

The second meaning of "evangelical" arose in the context of the Protestant Reformation in the sixteenth century and continues to function as a "rough synonym" for "Protestant."[2] Noll points out that this usage is still current in the Evangelical Lutheran Church in America; we can also recognize this meaning in other languages. For example, in Spanish, Latin American Protestant churches are often identified as *iglesias evangélicas.* In German, this sense of "Protestant" as synonymous with evangelical is present in Karl Barth's series of lectures on neo-orthodox theology given at the University of Chicago Divinity School and Princeton Theological Seminary some forty years ago. Barth published these lectures under the title, *Evangelical Theology: An Introduction.*[3] He meant to imply that the lectures were in the Protestant and Reformed tradition.

The third and fourth meanings of evangelical are associated with "the renewal movements of the eighteenth century and from practitioners of revival in the nineteenth and twentieth centuries," such as Charles Finney, D. L. Moody, and Billy Graham.[4] In this case, on the one hand, "evangelical" refers to those churches and movements that arise out of the Anglo-U.S. religious revivals of the eighteenth century, especially the denominations descending from John and Charles Wesley, George Whitefield, and Jonathan Edwards. On the other hand, and more significantly, today the term "designates a consistent pattern of convictions and attitudes."[5]

This fourth definition is generally the most common meaning today, though often we lack clarity about what those beliefs and attitudes are. Drawing on the work of David Bebbington, Noll identifies "four defining characteristics [that] are still generally valid," despite the inability to categorize U.S. evangelicals in monolithic terms. These elements include: 1) conversion; 2) the Bible as containing all spiritual truth; 3) "activism, or the dedication of all believers . . . to lives of service for God, especially manifested in evangelism . . . and mission"; and 4) "crucicentrism, or the conviction that Christ's death was the crucial matter in providing atonement for sin."[6] One or more of these four characteristics are, of course, held by a number of Protestants who would not consider themselves "evangelical" and who would interpret the beliefs in myriad ways. Moreover, Noll does not provide a definition for "evangelism," other than, "spreading the good news," a concern with which, again, many Protestants would agree, but with distinct ideas about the meaning and lived expression of this phrase.[7] Of course, this fourfold definition is further complicated by the "conservative" political commitments held by at least some rather prominent evangelicals apart from the basic set of theological beliefs. Today, these political commitments often seem to hold sway in the collective consciousness when hearing the term "evangelical." Images such as Pat Robertson's hateful pronouncements against leaders such as Hugo Chavez or Ariel Sharon and Jerry Falwell's denunciation of the purple Teletubby who carries a purse pervade our consciousness. Indeed, it is clear that such political commitments—albeit generally offered in less extreme forms—should be seen as a defining characteristic of contemporary evangelicalism, along with the pattern of beliefs.[8]

BASIC EVANGELICAL BELIEFS

1. Conversion
2. The Bible contains all spiritual truth
3. Activism that emphasizes evangelism and mission
4. The centrality of Christ's atoning death on the cross
5. Political commitments

In an attempt to more accurately understand evangelical Christians in North America, Noll examines a survey of three thousand persons in the United States and three thousand in Canada that used three methods of identification: 1) self-identification, 2) affirmation of one or more of the four characteristic beliefs, and 3) affiliation with denominations typically considered to be "evangelical" such as Adventist, Baptist, and Church of God.[9] His analysis of the findings suggests, "considerable differences result from defining 'evangelicals' as those who hold evangelical convictions when compared with the historic Protestant denominations where those beliefs have been most prominent."[10] In the United States, only about 19 percent of those polled would speak of themselves as "evangelical," yet some 36 percent affirmed the four beliefs.[11] Of those who self-identify as "evangelical," fully 74 percent affirm all four characteristic beliefs and 61 percent are affiliated with what Noll identifies as "evangelical Protestant" denominations.[12]

So when we raise the question of the relationship between evangelicalism and evangelism, we come face to face with the ambiguity that exists in the use of the term "evangelical." Although evangelicals consider evangelism to be an important component of their belief system, most mainline Protestants, including the historically black denominations in the United States, would not self-identify as "evangelical" (although, indeed, many would place themselves in the lineage of the eighteenth-century revivalists or affirm one or more of the four beliefs). We recognize that the political entanglements also dissuade some persons from identifying themselves as "evangelical."

Mainline Anglo and African American denominations would understand evangelism, defined as Noll does in terms of sharing or "spreading the good news," to be consistent with their beliefs and practices. If the survey is statistically representative of the larger U.S. population, then it becomes clear that over half of the Protestant Christians in the United States will not be comfortable with evangelism if it is associated with evangelicalism or the traditional approach taken by self-identified evangelicals. When we link the two terms theologically (and politically) as well as etymologically, the theology and practice of evangelism becomes meaningless or inappropriate for the majority of Protestant Christians in North America.[13]

The "Logic" of Evangelism

Adding to the problem is the fact that the body of literature associated with evangelism expresses, in large measure, an evangelical perspective in the contemporary sense (that is, generally based upon the four characteristics and associated political commitments).[14] For the purposes of grasping the contours of the problem, we can turn to *The Logic of Evangelism* by William Abraham as illustrative. Abraham aims to overcome the deficiencies of a narrow focus on evangelism rooted in a substitutionary theory of atonement (in which Jesus' death takes the punishment we deserve) and emphasizing conversion, or as simply a haphazard collection of practices, such as church growth, without a clear theological rationale. Yet, for the large number of Protestant Christians today who do not identify with contemporary evangelicals, his approach will not arrest the decline occurring in the contemporary church for four main reasons: 1) it posits the white, male, middle-class perspective as universal; 2) it uses scripture selectively; 3) it defines evangelism—an indisputably ambiguous term—in ways that promote the status quo rather than challenging it; and 4) it displays triumphalist tendencies. These features of evangelism, taken together, stand in opposition to the radically relational reality of God in Christ in the Holy Spirit and can serve to stifle renewal.

1. The Problem with Perspective

Abraham locates himself in the theological tradition that views Christian faith as based upon an internal logic or grammar that remains distinct from cultural contexts and, therefore, should be "countercultural." Yet, it is deceptive not to acknowledge that every theology and every era of church history demonstrates an important relationship to both the historical and the cultural contexts out of which it emerged and is awash in the particularities of human existence. For example, we generally read U.S. history through the narrative of manifest destiny and continental expansion, but when we view this same history through the eyes and culture of Native Americans, Mexicans, or African Americans, the story contributes a significantly different understanding. Alone, none can convey the "truth" of this history because one perspective is incomplete. Indeed, the fullest history would entail a "God's-eye" view that could bring together all peoples and the earth itself in telling the tale of how the United States became what it is today. Thus, when we ignore cultural and historical realities, we place blinders on the story and, as chapter 1 suggested, we then bracket out and set aside the very conditions that are now infecting the church and undermining its transformative power.

We need to take seriously our contemporary intellectual, social, and theological milieu if we wish to speak meaningfully and truthfully about God in Christ in the Holy Spirit revealed within the contexts of concrete, particular human history. In the nineteenth and twentieth centuries, human understanding was shaped by two important phenomena: historical consciousness and, more recently, cultural consciousness. Historical consciousness can be understood as the recognition, articulated initially by Wilhelm Dilthey, that human beings are "in" history and that this history forms a backdrop to our understanding and engagement of the world. For example, the history of slavery in the United States is not simply a past historical reality, but continues to have countless implications for our life together, despite those who would deny any ongoing racial divisions. Likewise, today no U.S. citizen could ignore the as-yet-unclear significance of September 11, 2001, to the conduct of life in this country. It has formed a backdrop to our lives that renders it more than simply past history. Indeed, the date, written as 9/11, has come to serve as a symbol for this historical reality. Yet, to Latin Americans, 9/11 evokes a very different history: the 1973 military coup in Chile, which brought General Augusto Pinochet and his brutal regime to power.[15] We are conscious of our history—or perhaps, histories—and the past, as it is transmitted to us, continues to shape the present and future (including the process by which the past is selectively interpreted, challenged, and reconceptualized over time).

Certainly Christians affirm this notion of historical consciousness when we recognize that the life, death, and resurrection of Jesus of Nazareth who is the Christ continues to shape and influence Christian life in the present and the future. The reality of Jesus Christ continues to take shape within communities of faith in our world today. Moreover, any theological position, whether formulated by the early ecumenical councils or by Christians in the twentieth century, are responses to particular circumstances arising within specific historical and cultural contexts of both church and society. For example, one cannot understand the early dialectic or crisis theology of Karl Barth without understanding the theological movements of orthodoxy and of classic liberalism that preceded him, as well as the intellectual shift generated by the Enlightenment and the profound impact of World War I. The emergence of James Cones's Black Theology would make little sense without the history and context of slavery in the United States and the civil rights movement in the 1960s. More recently, the body of literature and practices related to "church growth" can be attributed, at least in part, to the prominence of the managerial mindset in the latter half of the twentieth century.

A related, though more recent intellectual development is the rise of cultural consciousness, in which we recognize that multiple, overlapping cultural contexts impact how we engage and understand the world. As with history, we are "in" cultures, and they form the backdrop to our lives in tangible ways. For example, Eastern thought seeks harmony in the midst of tensions, while Western thought seeks to resolve tensions, that is, to find an answer that will eliminate opposing forces or positions. Within Christian communities, cultural characteristics influence life together in various ways. The members of an Anglo congregational church in New England will express their joy in the presence of God in different ways than a Hispanic Methodist church in the Rio Grande Valley. The hymns, the prayers, the participation of the people, the music, the language, the fellowship time, the outreach, and a host of other cultural realities will shape these expressions, yet they remain valid ways to worship and serve God in Christ in the Holy Spirit in the world. Where once Christians might have sought to reduce cultural difference and impose one culture as preferred over another, in recent years Christians have come to embrace and celebrate the variety of ways in which the Christian faith is expressed. We realize that the flourishing of difference is a gift of God who created the world in such spectacular variety.

Indeed, the gospel calls into question any claim that presents one perspective as universally valid or equally appropriate to a lobsterman in Maine, a Fortune 500 CEO in San Francisco, a hotel maid in Detroit, and a ninth-grader in El Paso who is a first generation immigrant. We need only look at the witnesses to Jesus of Nazareth who is the Christ to recognize how often Jesus is drawn out of his own social location—to speak in contemporary language—in order to acknowledge and affirm the experience of those at the margins of society and those whose lives are different from his own. Time and again, Jesus refuses to participate in the misguided privilege of the center to create and maintain edges of oppression and suffering—often just out of sight of those who live comfortable lives.

In one of the most extreme examples, Jesus is walking with his disciples when confronted by a Canaanite (Matt. 15:21–28) or Syrophoenician (Mark 7:24–30) woman. Jesus recognizes her as an outsider, as one who has no right to speak and request what he offers. Yet when she insists that he hear her perspective, Jesus is shocked into an awareness of his social location and how it functions to undermine, potentially, the flourishing of her life and that of her daughter. Had Jesus remained bound by his perspective and social location, the woman would have been put off by Jesus and closed to the message she had heard from some distance that had drawn her to him in the first place. Jesus is forced to examine his own position and is changed through his encounter with this woman and her experience of being "other" to Israel. The scriptures function to confront us with our own blind spots and challenge us to hear anew the liberating word of God, not to posit our own experience as universal and normative, a one-size-fits-all moral to the story. Because the living God has created us in history and cultures, they shape and form our lives in ways that both open us to God and can close us off to radical relationship and reorientation.

2. Scripture as a Resource for Evangelism

A second concern with contemporary works on evangelism is the use of scripture. While it is appropriate and important to begin with the scriptures and the gospel message, scripture is often used selectively to support a predetermined position or, at times, to provide the basis for a moralistic treatise. Either way, it is rendered into a caricature of the living, breathing, life-giving discourse of the gospel. Returning to our example, the *Logic of Evangelism* uses scriptural warrants selectively, which leads to a narrow reading of the biblical witnesses. Abraham bases his theological rationale and definition of evangelism on Jesus' message of the "kingdom of God." This biblical metaphor leads to placing eschatology, the "last things," at the center of evangelism.

Without question, eschatology and the news of the inbreaking realm of God are central to Jesus' message in the gospels, but they do not represent the full meaning and message of the gospel. Any biblical basis for evangelism that arises out of one text or one piece of the witnesses to Jesus Christ—whether the text of Matthew 28, the so-called "Great Commission," or the passages related to the "kingdom of God"—does not take the scriptures seriously enough. Theological reflection begins with and rests upon a broad and deep engagement of the biblical witnesses. God has chosen to reveal God's self in the scriptures, and we cannot choose which part of the revelation we will embrace and which we will ignore. Moreover, our theological reflection also includes reading from the margins and from different cultural contexts. Who we identify with in a parable, for example, often depends upon our social location and status in life. We are called to recognize distinct voices and patterns within the scriptures that bear witness to the good news in a full palette of shades and hues, rather than to read them in black and white.

Without a careful assessment of the fullness of the gospel message, evangelism, understood as "sharing the good news," will lack the fullness of the transformative power and liberating potential to which the scriptures testify. God seeks to liberate the whole web of creation from brokenness and transform it into the radical relationship of the new creation. For a theology of evangelism to be meaningful to the majority of Protestants and to contribute to the renewal of the church, we are called to wrestle with the scriptures as they bear witness to the full range of the birth, life, ministry, death, resurrection, and *parousia* of Jesus of Nazareth who is the Christ. We are called to illuminate what that message entails as best we can from within our conditions of brokenness. Indeed, while we can never adequately grasp and articulate the whole message revealed in and through Jesus of Nazareth because we are finite creatures, we are nonetheless compelled to seek the fullest possible understanding of God's self-revelation and the good news it entails, rather than choosing the portion of God's Word we find most appealing or conducive to our own theological commitments. The scriptures urge us to recognize that context influences our interpretation at any given point in history, even as the basic message, the good news in and of Jesus Christ, is the content of the New Testament as transmitted to us through the understanding of the Hebrew Scriptures. We cannot choose which portion of God's revelation we prefer and sidestep the rest; we must be open to encountering the whole and to seeing anew what we may have previously missed.

3. The Diverse Definitions of Evangelism

The third weakness in contemporary evangelism is that those who write about evangelism seem unable to agree upon a definition, suggesting the word's meaning is as narrow as proclamation to unbelievers, mere conversion to Christ, or even church growth, or as broad as the discipleship process itself. Evangelism can mean removing symbols of traditional Christianity or making attractive flyers to distribute in the neighborhood. It can mean "invite-a-friend-to-church Sunday." It has so many definitions that it seems unable to convey anything meaningful other than the need to arrest the decline of the church by whatever pragmatic solution appears on the horizon.

Abraham offers a "new definition" in response to these alternatives: evangelism is "initiation into the kingdom of God." Evangelism is designed "to admit that person into the eschatological rule of God through appropriate instruction, experiences, rites, and forms."[16] His intention is to shift the focus from initiation into the church to initiation into the kingdom of God, such that God is the primary agent, the church secondary, after which comes the evangelist, and, lastly, the person evangelized.[17] Abraham concludes that in order for the events to be construed as evangelism, "they must be causally related to the process of initiation into God's rule, and they must be governed by the intention to achieve this end."[18] Evangelism is thus conceived of as a practice of the church in relation to initiation or the beginning of the discipleship process. In a sense, it is ushering outsiders through the door to our house so they may become acquainted with the host.

It is not unusual in more traditional theological proposals, including evangelical theologies, to emphasize God's wholly otherness—what we would refer to as "transcendence." In his version of evangelism, Abraham emphasizes God's transcendence and sovereignty at the expense of a viable sense of God's immanence or presence among us, despite the fact that the reign of God is already in our midst. As Abraham argues, "[t]o be initiated into the rule of God is to encounter a transcendent reality that has entered history and to find oneself drawn up into the ultimate purposes of God for history and creation."[19] Our image here is that of being swept out of this world and into another one that is set apart and more pure or spiritual in nature. But when we emphasize transcendence, our life together becomes so focused on other-worldly-ness that it dissipates the meaning in and for the present and turns a blind eye and a deaf ear to the reality of the suffering and pain experienced by those who live within and under systems that oppress and marginalize.

By the same token, many megachurches and evangelicals that emphasize God's immanence tend also, at times, to ignore the pain and suffering around us, proclaiming that God blesses those who truly believe in Jesus Christ. As the *Prayer of Jabez* would claim, we need only to pray rightly and we will receive abundant material blessings. In this version of our relationship to God, we are given the image of Jesus implanted into each individual heart like a divine pacemaker, such that we are "one" with Jesus in a spiritual sense. If we are not careful, this "fusion" allows us to justify whatever we do as God's will because we are united with Jesus. We can seek worldly success in the name of God, who desires to "bless" us. Like a mysterious, unapproachable, wholly other God, the Jesus-in-my-heart version fails to take seriously the God who "makes a way out of no way," to use the powerful phrase of Dolores Williams in her reading of Genesis and the apparent hopelessness of Hagar's marginalization and abandonment.[20] Life in God is not a steady stream of progressively greater successes, richer riches, and higher highs, given by virtue of our mere confession of Christ. It is not an escape from the harsh realities of life on earth into a spiritual refuge. God is at work to bring justice and life to the four corners of the earth and to challenge us to change our ways and our sinful systems, which contribute to undermining the fullness of life in others and the flourishing of the whole of creation.

A transcendent, future-oriented eschatology, set apart from the world; an immanent, prosperity gospel in which we are given the good life now; or a gospel that takes us up into a spiritual realm apart from the world renders invisible both the presence of suffering and evil and the reality of Christian hope. Yet, it is precisely the hope that the gospel announces and to which it points that gives meaning to eschatology and to the practices of the Christian faith. It is hope that says God is at work in the world transforming suffering and evil, now and in the future. Faith without hope is meaningless, unless one seeks to preserve or promote as normative the status quo. If we do not wish to change, then we will not live hopeful lives. If we have everything now, we cannot hope. If we wish to escape from this world, then we will not act in the world as the body of Christ.

The importance of hope in evangelism is articulated by Mortimer Arias, who proposes that, "To be an evangelist is to be a sign of hope, a servant of hope, a minister of hope."[21] This means that we are to embody hope, as Jesus did, in three forms: annunciation, denunciation, and consolation. For Arias, this embodiment of hope, which is central to the reign of God, includes announcing the "gospel of the coming kingdom," as Martin Luther King Jr. did in proclaiming, "I have a dream" and inspiring others to work toward a profound transformation in U.S. society.[22] The embodiment of hope takes the form of a prophetic ministry of denunciation that denounces "anything, any power, any program, any trend which opposes God's purpose for humanity."[23] Arias suggests that any "human or social achievement will be penultimate—only the reign of God is ultimate and deserves our total loyalty. . . . We cannot commit ourselves to a program, to a national way of life, to a dream, or to a revolution as if they were the reign of God. But we can commit ourselves to the improvement and the transformation of society for the sake of the reign of God, in line with the reign of God."[24] He urges us to remember that this prophetic ministry of denunciation has led to the arrest, interrogation, imprisonment, torture, "disappearance," and death of countless Latin Americans, including the well-known case of Oscar Romero of El Salvador.[25] Finally, the embodiment of hope includes what Arias terms the "ministry of consolation," which is best described as compassion for those who suffer oppression, repression, human rights violations, and violence. He lifts up the defense of human rights as "a matter of witness and confession;" it is a "hope against hope," for millions, even billions, of persons across the globe.[26] To proclaim a message that ignores suffering, hope, and the urgent need for justice in today's world is far more likely to divert people from participating in the living God than to "initiate" them into God's reign.

Most definitions of evangelism contribute to reinforcing the status quo, not only by ignoring suffering, hope, and justice, but also by articulating hierarchical church models. In effect, they uphold power dynamics given to certain church authorities, rather than opening us to the transforming power of the gospel and God. In Abraham's definition of evangelism, we are presented with the idea of a process that intentionally brings people into the reign of God and the ecclesiology, the understanding of the church, which is the basis for it. Much of Abraham's book is devoted to describing the set of activities that will facilitate the desired goal of evangelism, identified as "initiation into the kingdom of God for the first time." His goal is to shift the conversation away from the evangelist who seeks the conversion of unbelievers and requires little more than the confession of faith, to an understanding grounded in the primacy of God and located in the worshipping community. Yet, despite this important and appropriate goal, Abraham's language and his descriptive account of the "activities" or practices, undermine the ecclesial reality he seeks to uphold and further.

The activities described by Abraham (that is, conversion, baptism, morality, creedal instruction, receiving gifts of the Spirit, and practicing the spiritual disciplines) are, at heart, an attempt to recover the catechumenate as central to initiation into God's reign. Further, Abraham seeks to establish the church in the patristic period as normative for the life of Christian faith and, therefore, for the ministry of evangelism. In his argument for the centrality of the Nicene Creed in this process of initiation, he argues that the early church (that is, the church in the third and fourth centuries) "found it essential to do at least three things to safeguard its intellectual treasures."[27] These actions were the closing of the canon, the development of the basic summaries of the faith that would form the basis of the creeds, and the establishment of an episcopate whose function was to preserve the teachings and authority of both canon and creed.[28] As a result, Abraham's ecclesiology represents a "high church," hierarchical model that fails to take seriously the Protestant Reformation and the priesthood of all believers. It places the work of sharing the gospel squarely on the shoulders of the authorities, the churchly power holders.

It is clear that not just anyone can administer or guide the "appropriate instruction, experiences, rites, and forms" described by Abraham.[29] Although he scarcely addresses a pragmatic plan for carrying out this set of activities, his nod to the regulatory function of the episcopate provides an important clue. Whatever is to happen must be carefully prescribed and controlled by those in positions of ecclesiastical power. The implications are significant. Not only do the leaders of any given church bear the brunt of the responsibilities for evangelism as initiation, but the work of evangelism is located within the church more than beyond its institutional walls. It is controlled by those who hold the power, and they prescribe what is authoritative and what is not, what is to be believed and not, who is to become a spiritual leader and not. Indeed, the power of the Spirit is as likely to be constricted in such models as to be present in a radically transforming way. After all, Jesus did not choose the powerful to begin the work of God, but ordinary people such as fishermen, tax collectors, and women who were generally marginalized from the teaching of the rabbis.

Is the answer to the decline of Protestant churches in North America a hierarchical ecclesiastical model as proposed by Abraham and others? Alternatively, should the minister become a "CEO" of the church in order to better manage the life of faith? Based upon the argument presented in chapter 1, namely, that the decline of the church is primarily spiritual in nature, reinforcing the structures of the institutional church—or relaxing them to a gelatinous mass—will not fix what ails Christian faith in the United States. Moreover, we are compelled to keep in mind that a radical spirituality is always deeply connected to the physical and material order that God created and continues to sustain. This criticism is not to suggest that the activities described by Abraham cannot function to encourage broader participation in the church, which is a desirable outcome; they certainly can. Yet, if wider participation among those who profess to follow Christ is our goal, then it would be wise to turn to the New Testament churches for guidance, rather than the later institutionalization of the Christian faith, and to open ourselves to the reorienting power of grace—a power that is disquieting and, at times, downright revolutionary.

David Bosch has argued that the "revolutionary nature of the early Christian mission manifested itself, *inter alia,* in the new relationships that came into being in the community. Jew and Roman, Greek and barbarian, free and slave, rich and poor, woman and man, accepted one another as brothers and sisters (Gal. 3:28). It was a movement without analogy, indeed a 'sociological impossibility.'"[30] We can describe this radical relationality as C. René Padilla suggests, in terms of a new identity. He contends that "the church is viewed in the New Testament as the solidarity that has been created in Jesus Christ and that stands in contrast to the old humanity represented by Adam."[31] The New Testament speaks of the removal of barriers that had previously caused separation and prevented solidarity or genuine relationship. It is a new reality, not the old society with its brokenness and division: "in Jesus Christ a new reality has come into being—a unity based on faith in him, in which membership is in no way dependent upon race, social status, or sex. No mere 'spiritual' unity, but a concrete community made up of Jews and Gentiles, slaves and free, men and women, all of them as equal members of the Christ solidarity—that is the thrust of the passage."[32] It is a reality in which the separation of spiritual and material, male and female, rich and poor is healed.

Padilla goes on to demonstrate that breaking down such barriers was no easier in the New Testament communities than it is today. Yet, that is exactly what Jesus did among those who gathered around him and what Paul advocated in his ministry to the Gentiles. Indeed, according to Bosch, the difference between the Jerusalem and Antioch churches in the first century can be described, at least in part, by this reduction of barriers: "The Antioch church's pioneering spirit precipitated an inspection by Jerusalem. It was clear that the Jerusalem party's concern was not mission, but consolidation; not grace, but law; not crossing frontiers, but fixing them; not life, but doctrine; not movement, but institution."[33] The church in Jerusalem understood itself as having a continuing allegiance to "Torah piety" and a mission to the house of Israel. Conversely, the "Antioch community was indeed amazingly innovative."[34] Although we cannot disregard contemporary criticisms of Paul's writings and theology, he nonetheless "provided the theological basis for the Torah-free self-definition of Gentile Christianity."[35] While avoiding separation into homogeneous churches, the early Christians forced neither Gentiles to follow the Mosaic Law nor Jews to endure practices that were offensive, but instead sought a harmony amid cultural differences.[36] As a result, we find evidence that the primitive church, the church of Pentecost, sought a level of sharing and participation unknown in later institutionalized forms: "the believers were 'together' (*epi to auto* in Acts 2:44), . . . they had 'all things in common' (2:44, 4:32), and . . . they were 'of one heart and soul' (4:32)."[37] It is remarkable today how many churches in the United States are homogeneous and widely disparate in their financial resources.[38] In fact, it is widely acknowledged that the eleven o'clock hour on Sunday morning is the most segregated time of the week in the United States. Are we really modeling the radical relationality of the gospel in our churches today?

What becomes clear when we open ourselves to the transforming grace of God in Christ in the Holy Spirit is that a new identity is formed, located in Christ rather than in the brokenness and separation fostered by worldly criteria. This new identity calls into question the ways of the world, the temptations of consumerism, individualism, and imperialism. It calls into question the status quo. It calls into question the use of power to separate and divide, rule over others, or shore up personal desire and gain. Instead, it points to a sharing of resources, a life together with others who are gathered from the four corners of the earth, with those who are not just like us but are the persons God created them to be. It is significant that in the early churches, "conversion was never a merely religious experience; it was also a means of becoming a member of a community in which people find their identity in Christ rather than in race, social status, or sex. The apostles would have agreed . . . that 'the point at which human barriers are surmounted is the point at which a believer is joined to Christ and his people.'"[39] We should not read this radical relationality as a loss of difference, but as a revolutionary embrace of it. Given that the earliest Christian communities expressed the reality of the body of Christ through a tangible solidarity found only in overcoming barriers that had previously created distinct hierarchies and separation according to human standards, any activities intended to "initiate" Christians today should seek the same. Any program of evangelism, of sharing the gospel, ought to work toward this new identity in Christ, in contrast to the brokenness, suffering, and injustice of life apart from God. In the following chapters, we will explore this identity, in order to more fully grasp the meaning and practice of the Christ character taking shape in us and in the world. Our goal is to move toward a more authentic embodiment of the good news of God in Christ in the Holy Spirit in the world.

Ultimately, we must suggest that the concept of "initiation" into God's reign cannot be prescribed via a certain set of activities as Abraham delineates them. While we might view these activities as "means of grace," to do so would expand the process beyond his framework to include the work of the church as a whole, since the means of grace cannot be limited to initiation. Yet, Abraham rejects a definition based upon a discipleship model, arguing that "[i]f everything is evangelism then nothing is evangelism."[40] The problem theologically is that we can never assess a person's spiritual condition; following a prescribed catechumenate can assure one's entry into the church as institution, but not into the reign of God. Even confession of faith and baptism never assure our relationship with God, for only God in Christ in the Holy Spirit can discern the deepest intentions of our human pronouncements and activities.

God's grace always precedes our understanding, and we receive faith, justification, and new life as children of God as sheer gift. The process of forming a new identity in Christ is a fluid reality in which a person's relationship to God can ebb and flow over a lifetime. In this sense, "evangelism" must continue over a lifetime since we have no guarantees as to when or how initiation into "God's rule" is accomplished. Moreover, as the contemporary cultural captivity of the church demonstrates, conversion—radical reorientation to God—is an ongoing process of repenting of our past and present missteps and our comfort with the status quo and returning to the revolutionary way of faith in Christ. We will return to the notion of "conversion" as reorientation in chapter 5.

4. The Triumphalist Tendency

So we are led to a final concern that is often found in evangelistic proposals: a triumphalist or an exclusionary approach to other religious traditions. In this understanding, not only is Christ the "only way," but evangelism uses imagery of "us" versus "them" and the language of victory, conquest, winning, and losing. Toward the end of Abraham's book, he provides a shorthand definition for evangelism—quite distinct from his proposal related to initiation—which is troubling: "for the purposes of this chapter we can define evangelism very broadly as any attempt to win others to allegiance to the Christian faith."[41] Or as he claims later in the chapter, "evangelists are given to winning people to a cause."[42] These phrases related to "winning" reverberate with a long history of Christian triumphalism and stir up painful memories of abuses of power and violence in the name of God by the institutional church over many centuries. They reverberate with false promises of televangelists proclaiming a prosperity gospel and fiery preachers on street corners proclaiming hell and damnation. They point toward assuming a certain way of life is normative and that those who don't follow are "losers," not "winners." It is, of course, a foray into judgment rather than love. It is a way of turning the good news into bad news. Despite Abraham's awareness of such past abuses, his language belies any such position of moderation and dialogue.

As people of God whose historical and cultural consciousness leads us to reject the language of "winning people" to Christ, we are challenged to seek a new language for evangelism, a more inclusive notion of the church as the body of Christ, and a more sensitive approach to "sharing the good news." If we can reconceive the language and imagery of evangelism, we may find it enables us to speak meaningfully to contemporary Christians and to others, bearing faithful witness to God. In a prophetic role, we can open ourselves to challenge the status quo, including—perhaps especially—our own privileged positions. The language of winning, of victory, of battle in the name of God for our cause is a language of divisiveness and conquest, rather than mutuality and love.

Ultimately, disentangling evangelism (as well as its synonym, "evangelization") from evangelicalism is a difficult proposition, complicated by the literature on evangelism and its advocacy of questionable practices that dilute the radicality of the gospel. Thus, we are led to suggest that the practice of evangelism can and should be named and conceived of in different ways. We have lost touch with the depths and heights of the gospel as well as the life-changing reality of God with us. A more authentic expression of the gospel in our culture and our lives is needed. But in order to move toward reconceiving evangelism in faithfulness to the gospel message, we need to understand where and how the word arose and what it was intended to convey. In other words, the biblical roots and the historical usage of the word "evangelism" help to further illuminate the task before us as people who follow the way of Christ.

WHERE IN THE BIBLE IS EVANGELISM?

Any attempt to define evangelism inevitably grows out of the biblical roots of the word. Contemporary writings on evangelism usually point to the relationship of the English word "evangelism" to the Greek verb *euangelizesthai* (*euangelizo* in the infinitive) and noun *euangelion*, typically in order to provide the basis for articulating the author's own definition of evangelism. Although the biblical understanding of *euangelizo* and *euangelion* represents the appropriate starting point for defining the term evangelism, the New Testament does not fully account for the definition articulated by many contemporary authors. Thus, the biblical cognates can help us to grasp the muddiness of our current understanding, but they cannot provide the clarity that is sometimes presumed to exist in the biblical text. In other words, when we turn to the Bible for a definition of evangelism, we do not find a clean correspondence to our current usage.

In a brief essay, New Testament scholar Craig Evans provides a helpful analysis of the lexical history of *euangelizo* and *euangelion* in classical Greek, the New Testament, and patristic writings. Although Evans's concern is to argue for the distinction between the role of the preacher and the pastor in the early church, his observations offer insights into the investigation at hand.[43] Evans argues that in later classical writings, *euangelion* had already taken on the meaning found in the New Testament of "good news," and *euangelizesthai* was used to represent the announcing of good news. He writes, "A typical scene would be one in which the excited herald comes running to the city gates with the 'good news' of victory or of the destruction of a fearful enemy."[44] Michael Green goes farther, arguing that the noun "was the word used *par excellence* to announce victory, victory over hostile forces, and, derivatively, of the thank-offerings given to the gods in gratitude for such victory."[45] Although neither author draws out its significance, the classical context suggests not only that the good news is announced publicly, but also that it has a distinctly public character or content because it is an announcement made to the community, sharing news that is beneficial to the whole community. Rather than an individual and private piece of news broadcast widely, the messenger breathlessly shouts of victory to and for all—a reality that remains true whether or not everyone hears the announcement or rejoices in it. In other words, the usage of *euangelizo* in later Greek writings suggests more than the fact that this announcement is made in public; it indicates the content of the message, itself, is inherently communal and social. The gospel is about a radically relational reality; when the Word is proclaimed and received, it forms us into a community in Christ.

In the New Testament, the meanings of *euangelizo* and *euangelion* become theologically significant. *Euangelizo* is variously translated, including: to proclaim, announce, bring, or share the good news. At times, the good news brought by the messenger refers to the *basileia* or reign of God, though a more general sense of announcing the good news is also present. Evans claims that *euange-*

lion, when used in the gospels and other New Testament writings, "refers to the victory that Christ won over sin, death, and satan. The gospel is the subject matter [proclaimed]."[46] In this context, the good news refers explicitly to the life, death, and resurrection of the one who is the Messiah and the meaning of this announcement. Michael Green's insightful study, *Evangelism in the Early Church,* points to the "variety and yet homogeneity of the contents ascribed to the evangel. . . ."[47] He continues:

> More specifically, they proclaimed the good news about "the kingdom," as Jesus had done. But this could very easily be misunderstood in the Roman Empire, as it was, for instance, at Thessalonica; so it is not surprising to find them more frequently preaching simply the person and achievement of Jesus as the good news. . . . The one who came preaching the good news has become the content of the good news![48]

Evans argues that in the epistles, the occurrences of *euangelizesthai* indicate "the meaning is to proclaim the gospel to unbelievers,"[49] yet the full range of occurrences in the epistles and New Testament are ambiguous on this point. In the New Testament, there are fifty-four occurrences of the verb *euangelizo*, and almost half (twenty-five) appear in Luke-Acts. In the Gospel of Luke, Jesus echoes Isaiah 42 as he announces that he has been anointed by the Spirit of the Lord, *euangelizesthai ptochois,* to bring good news to the poor (4:18). Again in Luke 7:22, Jesus announces that "the poor have good news brought to them" (*ptochoi euangelizontai*). In the parallel passage in Matthew 11:5—the only instance in which Matthew uses the verb euangelizo—Jesus likewise announces that "the poor have good news brought to them" (*ptochoi euangelizontai*). Matthew's single use of the verb is not modified by the addition of poor *in spirit.* This point is particularly significant when we call to mind the important distinction between Luke's and Matthew's version of the Sermon on the Mount (Luke 6:20, Matt. 5:3). Here, the use of *euangelizo*, in which the good news is brought to the poor, is not intended to suggest belief or unbelief and should not be construed as such. Rather, it points toward the content of the message, indicating the possibility of material, physical liberation in God; it is a message of ongoing hope rather than a call to immediate change. It is the good news of what God can do to remove the constraints that preclude their flourishing as human beings.

Paul, of course, orients his proclamation of the good news toward the Gentiles who do not know the living God in Christ in the Holy Spirit (for example, Rom. 10:15, Rom. 15:20–21). His use of *euangelizo* conveys the content of the gospel within the context of his mission to the Gentiles. We should understand that his focus on the Gentiles is a function of his calling rather than an indication that he would only proclaim the good news to unbelievers. For example, Paul writes of the gospel he proclaimed to the Corinthians, using the past tense to indicate a message that continues to be valid and to be shared among the believers (for example, 1 Cor. 15:1–2). He also uses *euangelizo* to indicate that Timothy "has brought us the good news of your faith and love" (1 Thess. 3:6). In other words, Paul's heavy emphasis on bringing the good news to unbelievers must be placed in the context of his ministry rather than taken as the breadth and depth of *euangelizo.*

Moreover, in the seventy-six occurrences in the New Testament of the noun *euangelion* (good news or gospel), forty-nine of them are found in Paul's letters. In the majority of these verses, Paul couples *euangelion* with other verbs that can represent the act of proclamation (for example, *peplerokenai*, Rom. 15:19; *katangellousin*, 1 Cor. 9:14; *kerusso* or *kerysso*, Gal. 2:2); as well as with verbs meaning to serve (*hierourgounta*, Rom. 15:16), share (*koinonia*, Phil. 1:5), and declare (*lalesai*, 1 Thess. 2:2), among others. In these multiple occurrences, Paul places the gospel into a wider net than that of simply announcing the good news to those who have not heard it. The fact that there are no occurrences of *euangelion* in Luke and only two in Acts most likely suggests a stylistic preference by the evangelist for the verb rather than the noun or, as Green notes, a preference for "Hebrew thought" as the verb "derives from Hebrew usage, Deutero-Isaiah in particular, but the Jews made no great use of the noun."[50] Although Mark does not use the verb *euangelizo*, he does use the noun eight times, four of which are animated by the verb *kerusso* (to proclaim or preach). Overall, throughout the New Testament writings, *euangelion* is frequently qualified, depending on the context, as the "gospel of God," "gospel of Christ," and "gospel of the kingdom," to name just a few. In sum, in the New Testament, *euangelion* is a multifaceted, multilayered word that takes on different nuances, depending on the context and the person who is writing.

More significantly, there were not one, but "three great words used for proclaiming the Christian message": not only *euangelizesthai*, but also *kerussein* (to proclaim) and *marturein* (to bear witness).[51] Green argues that the meaning of *kerusso* is equivalent to *euangelizomai* in the New Testament and that, once again, Jesus is "the absolute centrality of . . . what was proclaimed."[52] As for *marturein*, the biblical use of bearing witness can refer to either God bearing witness in terms of self-disclosure or to the people bearing witness to God in Jesus Christ and the Holy Spirit. Of significance is the fact that the Christians in the "apostolic Church were quite clear that God's gift of his Spirit was intended not to make them comfortable but to make them witnesses."[53] It is a startling claim that should lead us to ask: To what do our comfortable lives bear witness today? Finally, the Gospel of John makes the sometimes forgotten point that, "[o]nly God can bear adequate witness to God."[54] In sum, the fullest understanding of the "good news" lies in a complicated dance of meaning among these and other words and phrases in the writings of the New Testament. Clearly, we cannot simply track the use of *euangelizo* and *euangelion* if we hope to articulate the message of faith in God in Jesus Christ in the Holy Spirit.

Thus, we are compelled to ask a pivotal question about the New Testament language for sharing the gospel: How might we define or identify the content of this gospel, if it is the content and not the form that is primary? The answer is not easily articulated since there are different ways in which we can name and interpret the content of the good news or, in more traditional language, what God has done for us in and through Jesus Christ and the Holy Spirit and to which the scriptures testify. Although a thorough analysis of christology, soteriology, and atonement theories is beyond the scope of this study, such obvious doctrinal complexity leads us to recognize the significant impact the tradition and its myriad interpreters have had upon our identification of the gospel's basic content. We cannot escape from our historical and cultural consciousness, even as we might sincerely seek to do so. Nonetheless, our lives as Christians and our sharing of and participation in the gospel depend upon our grasp of the basic message.

THE CONTENT OF THE GOSPEL: Radical Relationship

Even as we acknowledge the inescapably interpretive move we must now make, the content of the gospel can be viewed as threefold, offering us the fullest, though not the final or complete, revelation of: 1) who God is, 2) what it means to be human, and 3) God's reconciling love or the inbreaking presence and future promise of the restoration of radical relationship for the whole of creation. A brief explanation of the three aspects of the gospel's content is indicated and warranted at this point, though in chapter 3 we will develop the content of the good news in relation to the basic shape of Godbearing in the world. In other words, our search for a more authentic form of sharing the gospel must begin with the content of God's revelation in Jesus Christ and the Holy Spirit.

The content of the gospel, the good news that is the subject of the New Testament writings, is located in the full narrative of the birth, life, death, and resurrection of Jesus Christ. Although it is not uncommon for one or two elements to be emphasized over others, the fullest understanding is found in the whole of the story of Jesus of Nazareth who is the Messiah. Although none of us is able to grasp the entirety of what God has revealed to us in and through Jesus Christ and by means of the Holy Spirit, it is nonetheless crucial that we not overemphasize the crucifixion at the cost of neglecting the profound meaning of the incarnation. Likewise, to emphasize the ministry of Jesus of Nazareth and to pay scant attention to the resurrection empties the cross of significance and leads us toward anthropocentricism. The whole of the gospel in the context of the whole of the scriptural witnesses, both Hebrew and Greek, provides us with the deepest understanding of God's revelation in history. Yet, this revelation in Jesus Christ is expressed most powerfully and succinctly in the reality of the incarnation, in the divine assuming finite form, for it is here that the fullness of God, the fullness of humanity, and the fullness of relationship are encapsulated, written in shorthand to provide the outline of a mystery beyond our ability to comprehend as finite creatures. We glimpse the fullness but remain limited by our finitude and incompleteness.

When we ask about the content of this revelation, first, we find that from the Christian perspective, we are given a glimpse of the nature of God. This is what we mean when we confess the full divinity of Jesus Christ. In and through Jesus we are able to grasp the love, justice, power, compassion, righteousness, inclusiveness, hospitality, peacefulness, boldness, and openness of God in a clearer light. Yet, as finite creatures we are unable to know God *in se*. Now we see in a mirror dimly; now we know only in part, as 1 Corinthians 13:22 expresses. Like Moses, we are able to see only the back of God pass by as we hide ourselves in a crevice of the rock (Exod. 33:17–23). Finitude simply cannot bear the fullness of divinity. For example, when we experience the suffering of others in close proximity to us—the horrors of September 11, 2001, or the aftermath of Hurricane Katrina—we are almost immobilized by the heaviness of the sorrow and pain we feel out of compassion for those most directly affected. Yet, the God of compassion knows and shares in every ounce of suffering in the whole of creation at any given millisecond: every person, every animal, every plant, every cell of creation. Wherever creation cries out in pain, sorrow, agony to the living God, the ears of God's heart hear and share in that suffering. What human being could bear the fullness of the world's suffering for an instant and not be crushed under the weight? It is simply impossible for us to fully grasp the nature and reality of the Triune God. Traditionally, theology has claimed the finite is incapable of the infinite; it is a logical and physical impossibility to know God fully. Yet, because we are fully known, because God knows what we are capable and worthy of knowing, God has revealed the heart of God's self to human beings in the birth, life, death, and resurrection of Jesus of Nazareth who is the Christ. The gospel message points to God in Christ in the Holy Spirit and enables us to place our faith, hope, and love in the nature and promises of God.

The remarkable thing about the gospel message is that, even as it reveals to us the nature and promises of God, it also reveals to us what it means to be human, to be fully human as God created us to be. As creatures who live in and contribute to a world that is not as it should be, a world that is filled with evil, sin, suffering, pain, and death rather than the goodness, love, justice, and life of God, we cannot understand by means of the natural world and order of things who we are called to be as creatures before the Holy God. Christian faith speaks in mythical terms of the goodness of creation followed by a disruption of that goodness. Langdon Gilkey explains the second creation story in Genesis 2 and 3 as a mystery that, above all, reveals evil and suffering came "after" not "with" creation.[55] From within the brokenness of existence, we are unable to comprehend what it is to be fully human as God created us to be. Yet, God has revealed to us the fullness of humanity in the incarnation. In this fully human one, Jesus of Nazareth who is the Christ, we find the prototype for human life, not in terms of any particular physical characteristics, but in terms of radical relationship, solidarity, and mutuality with God, others, and the whole of creation, including the self. The gospel message points to the fullness of humanity—love of God, love of neighbor, love of the created world for which we are to exercise careful stewardship, and the love of one's self in a way that is neither selfish nor selfless, but properly self-concerned, caring for the integrity of the spiritual, physical, emotional, and intellectual dimensions of our humanity. Love in life-giving relationships, not judgment, not domination, not subjugation, not selflessness is the fullest expression of human creatureliness. In this sense, we find that the gospel message is a life-centered discourse pointing toward the flourishing of the whole of creation. The gospel tells us that life in its fullness, including the flourishing of human life, is a real possibility, despite the presence of brokenness.

Finally, in the incarnation we see evidence of God's reconciling love. In the restoration of radical relationality through the mysterious interweaving of the fullness of God and the fullness of humanity, we are given a glimpse of the new creation. Within the brokenness of existence, God initiates the process in which the whole of creation will be restored to its God-given goodness, harmony, justice, and peacefulness. The gospel message announces that, in Jesus of Nazareth who is the Christ, God has reconciled with "fallen" humanity and that we have the hope of restoration to the fullness of life, which means nothing less than the fullness of relationship for the whole of the cosmos. In the scriptures, we are given glimpses of the promised restoration of all things: the lion lying down with the lamb, the child playing on the adder's den, humanity walking with God in the cool of the evening, the eradication of death—the ultimate disruption of relationship. Although we live in the midst of almost unbearable brokenness, in the gift of the incarnation God reconciles God's self to the human creature.

Traditional theology has held that the atonement, God's reconciliation with humanity, takes place in the crucifixion; yet, we cannot ignore that a radically relational reality occurred in the incarnation. It is a relationship that we can scarcely grasp. The incarnation has long been debated and the subject of various "heretical" positions that have denied either the humanity or the divinity of Jesus, based upon the logical impossibility of such relationality being present in one concrete point. Yet in this one historical event, the radically relational way of the living God broke into existence and continues to illuminate God's message that out of the separation and division within which the universe now exists, a relationality has irrupted that will enable the whole of creation to flourish. Out of the self-centered and power- and wealth-hungry individuality of human society, genuine community has been implemented. This is a new creation first witnessed in the infant born to peasant parents, stranded far from home without a support system, in the bleakness and barrenness of winter when the evidences of life seemed most hidden, to a father who knew this child was not his own and a mother who was little more than a piece of property within the patriarchal society of first-century Palestine.

Yet out of this marginalized and broken beginning, a radically relational reality dawns: wise men and shepherds, sheep and cattle, Jews and Greeks, rich and poor, male and female, and the light from a brilliant star gather as one in a shabby stable to bear witness to this new creation and to share in the glory and wonder of the living God. The rich lay their treasures at the feet of the indigent; the powerful discover a humble new king; and those who have minimal voice and rights—a woman and a child—take center stage. The good news begins not with the claim that Christ died for us, but with the incredible message that God lived for us! God became flesh and entered into relationship with humanity, making no claims to power and privilege, but asking only to be loved and cared for. God's way is the way of love and gentleness, as Paul so eloquently expresses in 1 Corinthians 13. The human love of power, privilege, domination, accumulation, judgment, control, and violence ultimately forces the radically new creation that is born in Bethlehem to the abandonment, hatred, and suffering of the cross. The cross of death is the human way; the incarnation and the resurrection of life is the way of the divine.

As we more closely investigate the biblical witnesses to the gospel in chapter 3, this threefold content will come into sharper focus, undergirded by the voices and narrative of scripture. At this point, we are led to recognize that the fullness of the gospel message cannot be narrowed to one piece of good news about God or humanity or the relationship between God and humanity; rather, it involves all three and, even more, involves the restoration of the whole of creation. Unfortunately, traditional evangelism has tended to narrow the conversation and lose sight of the breadth and depth of the revelation in Jesus of Nazareth who is the Christ, as revealed in the scriptural witnesses from Genesis to Revelation. Our task is to develop a more authentic way forward. As we turn now to a brief history of the emergence of the word and practice of "evangelism," the limits we have imposed upon the work of God in Christ in the Holy Spirit in the world will become clearer and will enable us to move beyond the "muddiness" of evangelism today.

A BRIEF HISTORY OF "EVANGELISM"

During the early institutionalization of the church, as doctrine and practices developed, the Greek words related to the gospel, *evangelizo*, *kerussein*, and *marterein*, among others, underwent further refinement and interpretation. The process of translation into myriad languages and cultural expressions, which continues today, began to stretch and shape and reframe the biblical words. Evans notes that "[t]here are only five occurrences of *euangelizesthai* in the apostolic fathers" and the noun, *euangelion*, "is found 19 times in the writings of the fathers with no reference to 'preaching the gospel' to the congregation."[56] Here we cannot help but notice along with Evans that the word was already disappearing from common usage in Greek and Latin by the fifth century.

In fact, rather strikingly we find that, in English, the word evangelism did not enter into usage until the nineteenth century. Mendell Taylor opens his lengthy study, *Exploring Evangelism,* by highlighting that,

> The word evangelism was slow in making an appearance in the vocabulary of the Christian world. . . . Although Biblical writers introduced the term, it failed to become meaningful enough to be used in Christian circles until the nineteenth century. . . .
>
> In 1850, one of the first books was published with the term evangelism in its title. The author was Charles Adams. The work was entitled *Evangelism in the Middle of the Nineteenth Century.*[57]

Alternatively, Bosch suggests the term gained prominence around the turn of the twentieth century due to the slogan from the Edinburgh World Missionary Conference of 1910, "The evangelization of the world in this generation."[58] In either case, the late origin of the word evangelism in the English language is not disputed, and we should recognize the implications of this late introduction.

How, then, did English-speaking Christians refer to *euangelion* prior to the nineteenth century? The *Oxford English Dictionary* provides a helpful insight. While the entry on evangelism is brief and represents a short history of usage, the entries on both "gospel" and "mission" are extensive, dating back well into Old English. Particularly significant is the etymology of "gospel," which enters into English as the translation of *euangelion*, good news or good tidings:

> When the phrase *gód spel* was adopted as the regular translation of evangelium, the ambiguity of its written form led to its being interpreted as a compound, *gŏd-spel,* f. GOD + *spel* in the sense of "discourse" or "story." The mistake was very natural, as the resulting sense was much more obviously appropriate than that of 'good tidings' for a word which was chiefly known as the name of a sacred book or a portion of the liturgy.[59]

This etymological background indicates that, for generations, the primary word for *euangelion* in the English language was simply "gospel" or as the OED suggests, "God-story." Thus, our evidence trail leads clearly to the recognition that evangelism is a word without a long history of usage and, as we have previously seen, exists as only one among several biblical expressions related to sharing the gospel message.

Why did Evangelism Emerge in Modernity?

In light of the relative newness of the word evangelism, there are four distinct possibilities related to its appearance in the English language during the modern era. These options are that evangelism was associated with: 1) the rise of an entirely new practice within the Christian faith; 2) the recovery of a Christian practice that was rooted in the early church but was subsequently lost or neglected; 3) the renaming of an ongoing practice of Christian communities; or 4) the response to certain historical and cultural realities of modernity and was, therefore, pragmatically occasioned. Each of these possibilities deserves a brief consideration.

The first position—that the emergence of the word evangelism coincided with the introduction of a new practice into the Christian faith—can be dispensed with fairly quickly. Since we find a biblical basis for the broad practice of sharing the good news, as well as a long, though not always commendable history in which the Christian faith spread from one continent to another, few would argue that the church had lacked a sense of this task until the modern era. Indeed, had evangelism suddenly opened a new practice, we would expect to encounter clarity, rather than muddiness, in its definition. Yet, as Bosch indicates, the literature on "evangelism" contains one hundred or more different definitions, a phenomenon that is exacerbated by the widespread confusion about the relationship of evangelism to the Christian practice of "mission."[60]

If evangelism did not initiate a new practice within the Christian church, then could it have arisen in order to recover a lost practice? This second possibility is intriguing, given the fact that the word fell out of use over the centuries. Yet, we are hard pressed to identify anything in particular that was recovered in the practices and language related to the word's emergence in the nineteenth century. Serious scholars and practitioners of the Christian faith lament the more recent slew of "evangelistic" practices such as church growth and marketing methods that lack a theological and scriptural basis, and in fact, these more "secular" techniques only arise later in the twentieth century. Thus, it is difficult to argue that the basic notion of attending to the church's mission to share the gospel was a renewal of some practice, though perhaps we could point toward a renewed *emphasis* on the sharing of the gospel message.

As we turn to the third and fourth possibilities for the word's emergence, both appear as viable explanations. In suggesting previously that evangelism might represent a renewed emphasis by the Christian church on sharing the gospel message, the renaming of a practice seems plausible, especially when we consider the ongoing confusion and uncertainty about the relationship of evangelism to mission. Is evangelism the same as mission, related to mission, or a distinct activity apart from Christian mission?[61] At times, those who distinguish between evangelism and mission argue for a spiritual priority to the gospel message: evangelism is about spiritual liberation and transformation, and mission relates to the material and physical dimension of transformation.

Yet to separate the spiritual from the material is to divide and conquer the wholeness of God's creation. I join many contemporary authors who find this separation to be theologically untenable.[62] To suggest the "soul" must be given priority over the "body" is to enter into the long history of Christian thought that, at times, led to "heresies" such as gnosticism and docetism. Christians affirm that God created us as embodied, finite creatures rather than ethereal spirits. We also affirm that what God created in the beginning was deemed "very good," not something fundamentally flawed and designed to be left behind. The incarnation expresses powerfully the goodness of the human body, since God could not have assumed flesh if it were inherently evil or defective. God cannot do that which is contrary to God's nature; therefore, God could not join God's self to evil.[63] Indeed, Christians have proclaimed the resurrection of the body since the earliest days of the church, not simply the resurrection of the soul.[64] While it is intellectually incredible to provide explanation for the reconciliation and restoration of the physical, material body, the doctrine of bodily resurrection impels us to care for and attend to the physical and material world that God created. To do otherwise is to seek to be God-like, to be infinite spirit, rather than finite, material creature. To embrace faith in God in Christ in the Holy Spirit is to embrace our human embodiment and the physical realities of the whole of creation. When we do not, the theological errors are many: passivity, the abuse of bodies, the degradation of nature, the squandering of precious resources, and so forth.

Indeed, the argument that evangelism relates to spiritual renewal and that mission tends to the physical has been criticized by many scholars from a variety of theological perspectives. Samuel Escobar, for example, emphasizes the process by which evangelicals are rediscovering the "holistic" nature of Christian mission: "The gospel's dramatic influence [among the apostles] was seen not only in how it transformed individual lives but how it affected social structures."[65] Noting that "Latin Americans, Africans, and Asians, as well as African Americans and Latinos in the United States, insisted that evangelism and mission could not be carried on in faithfulness to biblical standards unless this holistic dimension was taken into account,"[66] Escobar goes on to describe various evangelism conferences, such as the Latin American Congress on Evangelism in 1969, which critiqued the division between evangelism and social action and "concluded that true evangelism could not take place without adequate reference to the social and political context within which it is done."[67]

Similarly, Arias describes the emergence of Base Communities, *communidades de base,* in Latin America as a model for discipleship and evangelization. He writes that these Christian communities "do not separate evangelization from social action—maybe most of them do not know the difference, not being used to our neat definitions and dichotomies. . . . Evangelization in this kingdom perspective is natural and effective. It is not only verbal proclamation, but also the incarnation of the gospel in the lives of the people and the community."[68] In fact, Arias concludes with a powerful claim that in joining spiritual and material transformation, "the church can reach a new authenticity, a new credibility. . . ."[69] The wholeness or integrity of the human being is a key to how conversion should be understood. Pointing to the theology of Gustavo Gutiérrez, Arias explains that

> conversion has been a long process for the present generation of Christians in Latin America. They were at first "unaware" and "unconcerned" about the situation of the people, and made a radical separation between the religious and the secular, this life and next. Then they began to be "aware" of the suffering and the problems of the people and tried to develop helping programs by applying some social principles from the church. They moved into politics to try to change the situation through legislation. Gradually, through more rigorous analysis of poverty and exploitation and their sources in international and national structures, these Christians became "radicalized." They made "the major discovery of our generation": the discovery of the "other"—the neighbor. And this was a true conversion experience.[70]

Feminist theologians have likewise critiqued this sort of spiritual-material dualism and other binary pairs like heaven-earth, male-female that often lead to hierarchical orderings and, in patriarchal societies, viewing women as inferior and "closer to nature."[71] Sallie McFague, for example, has critiqued the disparagement of the body in Western culture, including within Christianity, and asserted that "Christianity is the religion of the incarnation *par excellence.* Its earliest and most persistent doctrines focus on embodiment: from the incarnation (the Word made flesh) and christology (Christ was fully human) to the eucharist (this is my body, this is my blood), the resurrection of the body, and the church (the body of Christ who is its head)."[72] The embodied language of Christian faith leads McFague to conclude that all bodies, both living and inert, are created by God and deserving of care and respect. Similarly, in delineating the contours of a "theology of embodiment," Elisabeth Moltmann-Wendel summarizes the feminist approach to the body-spirit dichotomy: "A theology of embodiment mistrusts all abstract spirituality which is dissociated from the body, life, earth, and social relationships. . . . Disembodiment is lovelessness. Insecurity, coldness, power and weariness are hidden behind abstraction."[73]

When we recognize that a spirit-body or spirituality-physicality dichotomy is inconsistent with the Christian faith and largely attributable to the Western philosophical tradition, we are unable to separate evangelism from mission as representing two separate religious phenomena. Yet, we cannot ignore the possibility that this renaming of mission or dividing it into the spiritual and physical aspects may well have been intended by nineteenth-century writers. In the twentieth century, there is evidence to suggest that evangelism became more prominent as at least some evangelicals sought to distinguish themselves from mainline Christians with regard to the question of separating the spiritual from the material, the personal from the social.[74] At the same time, however, it is argued that some mainline Protestants and Catholics preferred the term evangelism or evangelization to "mission," due to the violent and imperialistic history of missions, especially in the colonial era. Perhaps both aspects of "renaming" furthered the usage in more recent years. Nonetheless, it does not entirely account for the emergence of the term in the nineteenth century as a renewed emphasis on a Christian practice and leads us to consider the historical and cultural considerations that might have occasioned the introduction of evangelism.

The influence of historical and cultural realities regarding the rise of the term evangelism and the accompanying emphasis on sharing the gospel is an intriguing question, deserving critical attention. Indeed, one could write a book on this particular aspect of evangelism. In brief, however, it is important to note some of the more obvious and likely influences on the emergence of evangelism in the nineteenth century, though these possibilities are not necessarily commensurable explanations. First, the predominant theology of the age was classic liberal theology in which an increasing emphasis was placed upon the human being, the capacity of reason, individual autonomy, and the potential for moral improvement, if not perfection. For those who began to view this trend as problematic, a return to the biblical message of the human need for God's grace might be a reasonable response. Indeed, it could have been viewed as crucial to the survival of the church, given the growing "liberation" of human beings from various social authorities, including the church. Yet, here it is interesting to note that Karl Barth, who challenged classic liberal Protestantism, did not embrace "evangelism":

> In the folklore of the ecumenical movement, there is a story about the annual visit of graduate students at the Ecumenical Institute in Bossey to the great theological patriarch in Basel—Prof. Karl Barth. Students were allowed to put questions to Barth. . . . Students: "Sir, what is the difference between mission, witness and evangelism?" Barth: "Mission is always mission of the church, witness is always witness to Jesus Christ, and evangelism is an invention of D. T. Niles."[75]

Second, we could point toward the onset of the industrial revolution and the rise of transportation and communication technologies that simplified the spread of the gospel, thus generating a new excitement over the possibilities for reaching people. Third, surely the rise of denominational mission boards and the emergence of the social gospel could have spurred others to respond by emphasizing the proclamation of the gospel, the "conversion" of souls, rather than attending to social needs. Moreover, on this note, recognizing that many mission boards were created by women who came to wield considerable power through those societies and boards, despite their lack of legal and ecclesiastical rights, some men might have felt an urgency to "take back" the work of the gospel through "evangelism." During the first half of the twentieth century, major denominations, including the Disciples of Christ, Presbyterians, and Southern Baptists, developed evangelism boards.[76] Then, too, we cannot ignore major figures such as Charles Finney, whose influence on revivalism was considerable. In March 1930, he established a magazine, the *New York Evangelist* "devoted to the objective of promoting revivals."[77] Perhaps amid the revivalism of the late nineteenth and early twentieth centuries, the term came increasingly to be accepted as a means of identifying their emphasis on public preaching and public "decision" for Christ.

Although today most publications dealing with the theory and practice of evangelism dispute a definition that restricts evangelism to the proclamation of the gospel, it is not inappropriate to suggest that the original usage of evangelism, in fact, did rest largely in the notion of proclaiming the gospel and seeking "conversion" to Christ.

The contemporary protests and arguments to expand the definition of evangelism would indicate that the nineteenth-century practice and language is no longer feasible or, perhaps, inappropriate for one or more reasons. Yet, those like William Abraham who advocate placing evangelism in a larger framework either establish limits to the practice (so as not to equate it with mission or discipleship) or simply agree that it is synonymous with mission. Admittedly, all theological language fails to capture fully the reality of God and the *Missio Dei* among us, whether mission, evangelism, witness, or any other dimension of life in God. Yet, some theological language is more sensitive to the nuances of meaning when dealing with the faithfulness of and to God. If it no longer conveys any particular and meaningful activity of the church, perhaps the usefulness of the term "evangelism" has run its course.

So we are left with the muddiness of evangelism. We cannot turn to the Bible for an exact definition; the Christian tradition has focused on mission, and the history of evangelism is a short one; the contemporary connotations are dominated by the evangelical perspective. Yet many churches and Christians continue to stress evangelism, acknowledging that most denominations in North America are declining. While mission remains a viable field with a wealth of significant literature, in the chapters that follow I will suggest a third way, a way that opens us to a deeper and more wholistic spirituality. It highlights the need to embrace new language related to the witness and lived expressions of the person who has faith in God in Christ in the Holy Spirit, in accordance with the gospel message. In light of the problems of meaning associated with evangelism and the term, mission, we will travel a different path, illuminating the meaning of sharing the gospel reconceived as Godbearing.

three JESUS, THE PROTOTYPICAL GODBEARER

If our sense of the church and what it means to be faithful to God in the world is misled by the language of evangelism, then we need to reawaken our senses and return to life in God in the deepest and richest meaning of life together. Evangelism has been conceived in ways that hold at bay the revolutionary power of grace, and we are urged to reclaim a more authentic and life-transforming expression of the gospel. For too long our identity has been formed by all manner of things except the deep Spirit of God. We have pursued our national agenda in the name of God. We have pursued our self-improvement in the name of God. We have pursued our desire for treasures and pleasures in the name of God. We have pursued our version of "church" at the expense of radical relationship with God. Consequently we have too seldom opened ourselves to the radical love of God that transforms us in ways we can scarcely imagine.

In this chapter, we explore more carefully what turning to God and opening ourselves to grace looks like in the midst of a broken world. After addressing the notion of the Christ character within the context of the radical relationality of God, we will enter into dialogue with the witnesses of the scriptures in order to bring to light the nature of Godbearing. Godbearing is expressed in the world as bearing the renewed image of God within, bearing God to others, and bearing with God the suffering of others. As we search the scriptural witnesses to Jesus of Nazareth who is the Christ, this basic shape or pattern will begin to emerge before us. It will enable us to reclaim what it means to share and live the good news of God in Christ in the Holy Spirit in the world.

THE CHRIST CHARACTER AND THE RADICAL RELATIONALITY OF GOD

When we accept the calling of grace to follow the way of Jesus Christ in the world, we begin to live according to different standards and to pursue new ways of being in the world. No longer bound solely to the world's pleasures and treasures, we begin a journey from brokenness toward wholeness. We begin to discover what it means to be fully human—not as we have imagined we might be via fortune, fame, power, and pleasure, but as God intends us to be. If we turn to the witnesses of the God-story, we find page after page testifying to the brokenness of our existence. We are not in relationship with God as we were created to be. Nor are we rightly related to others, to ourselves, or to God's creation. From our outstretched hands at the tree in the middle of the garden to the messages we receive as we sit among John's seven churches, we know ourselves to be beyond the garden and not yet able to enjoy the new heavens and earth in their fullness. In between we are assaulted with the lovelessness, brokenness, and the spiral toward the dusty destination of death, which characterizes human existence.

The reality of human life is that we find ourselves struggling against forces that undermine wholeness. While many advertisements persuade us to think that certain products or services can enable us to live nearly perfect lives, the daily news reveals that we are unable to insulate ourselves against pain and destruction. Great political and social leaders like John and Robert Kennedy and Martin Luther King Jr. are cut down in their prime, dashing dreams of the new Camelot. One of the world's most beautiful women, Diana the Princess of Wales, goes from fairy-tale wedding to self-loathing, divorce, and an untimely end, crushed in the darkness of a tunnel. Our next door neighbor is diagnosed with cancer and dies in a few short weeks. A Salvadoran man dies in the New Mexico desert trying to cross the border to the promised land, succumbing to dehydration or shot by a band of vigilantes claiming to protect life, liberty, and the pursuit of happiness. We fight against one another, devising more cataclysmic ways of annihilating others, even as the old-fashioned ways of death continue to stalk us. We fight against ourselves, trying hard to become something or someone we are not and cannot be. We fight against creation, constantly bemoaning the passing of time, depleting the earth's resources, struggling to find a space of our own that is sufficient for our burgeoning collection of possessions. We fight against credit card debt that squanders our restful sleep and strains our bonds. We fight against the captivating and unrelenting lure of drugs, alcohol, sex, gambling, shopping. We are never satiated. We who call ourselves Christians fight against one another, often claiming that we are the ones who know God, and everyone else is wrong. Everywhere we turn we find broken relationships, broken lives, and broken hearts. Human life as we know and experience it can only be categorized as a series of unwelcome and painful breaks interrupting our pursuit of happiness and wholeness.

Yet, when a moment of sheer grace or an interval of bliss encircles us, we know that there is more to life than the constant struggle to live in the midst of the gnawing knowledge of the end that daily draws us nearer. The cry of a newborn baby, the blossoming of spring, words of forgiveness spoken in sincerity, the deep experience of God's nearness—all of these and so many other moments give us hope and fill us with possibility. We are drawn to life and to the fullness of relationships. Of all the desires that demand our attention, the desire for life abundant is, perhaps, the first and last of all. At the edges of birth and death, the simple and all-consuming drive for life becomes primary. In between, we yearn to live in connection to God, ourselves, others, and creation.

But no matter how much power or wealth we may have, no matter how much we might accomplish in life, we are grasped by the truth of our existence: we remain on a headlong course toward death. And death is the ultimate condition of brokenness. All relationships cease, save the relationship of dust to dust and the intermingling of dust with the cosmos. We are in the process of becoming dust no matter how much we try to believe we are the most important form of life on earth. This awareness of the painful and tragic dimension of existence is what we are identifying as brokenness. If Christian faith fails to attend to this dimension of existence, we will not articulate the gospel message in terms fitting to our lived realities. We may try to ignore any implication of brokenness or seek to deny its presence in our lives, but when we are forced to confront and ponder the meaning of life, we are capsized by the flood of broken fragments that compose our lives. Anyone who lives amid poverty, homelessness, chronic disease, war, or other unyielding weights cannot imagine away his hunger or thirst, her shivering or wasting flesh, or the ferocious roar of roadside bombs and stinging bullets.

Indeed, the gospel message urges us to acknowledge who and what we are when left to our devices, dreams, and schemes. We are called to remember the widow, the orphan, and the stranger among us and to lay down our lives of comfort for the sake of God's way taking shape in the world. We are confronted with the futility of trying to fill our lives with money, power, pleasure, or even ever more self-abasement, and the sense that something is missing lingers. Only when we open ourselves increasingly to the grace of God, when we enter into and live out of the God-story, do we begin to recognize how God moves in and through the creation. Only then are we able to follow the Spirit's lead in the dance of grace. Over time, as we respond to the offer of grace, we find that our lives and hearts become reoriented toward God, others, ourselves, and the whole of creation. Over time, by grace we are shaped more sharply into the form of the Christ character and express this identity through Godbearing in the world.

The Christ character is the fullest expression of what it means to be human. In turning toward radical relationship with God, self, others, and creation, we begin to realize our truest nature, as exemplified in Jesus of Nazareth. It is an identity unlike the kind of personhood projected and imaged by the larger society. Our society with its image-making machinery urges us to focus on behavior and self-actualization, to improve the outer person with the right "look" or attitude. We are impelled by society to seek elements of a supposed "good life" that often undermine the flourishing of other persons or the created world. We have come to believe that image, power, the right connections, money, and a beautiful body are just about everything. Much of the time, we would rather look good than be good. Yet deep within our hearts, we often yearn to be George Bailey in *It's a Wonderful Life,* who ultimately discovers how thoroughly connected he is to a much larger reality than the self-image he has projected. He discovers that a good life is found in a series of small, seemingly ordinary acts in each moment of his life, acts that weave him and others together into a remarkable, responsible community.

When we are open to God in Christ in the Holy Spirit, the Christ character takes shape within us and begins to reorient our very being to the reality of God, to the possibility of wholeness in a world filled with brokenness and division. It illuminates our vision and orients or directs our attention away from the desire for self-actualization through receiving more or giving ourselves away until nothing remains. The light that shines within the human spirit cannot be manufactured by swallowing the right vitamins or enjoying the finest spa treatment. It cannot be gained by securing the lowest mortgage for the biggest house or developing the smartest strategy for portfolio diversification. It cannot be obtained by becoming the pastor who works eighty hours a week and still frets about the time she has spent on herself, or the person who agrees to participate in another volunteer activity because he has not yet given away all of his free time.

To the contrary, life takes shape in the depths of our being as the Christ character begins to enliven our existence within the web of relationships that characterizes the created order. We begin to grasp that who we are is fundamentally about our openness to participate in a larger reality than our immediate needs and desires, to live within a delicate harmony of giving and receiving life. To be a person of Christian faith is to be a member of the body of Christ. It is an inescapably communal reality, in which a balance between giving and receiving surrounds and infuses us, challenging us, holding us accountable, comforting us, and enabling us to live more fully as people of God. The Christ character is inescapably communal and, we might say, dialogical, for when we accept the gift of faith, we enter into renewed relationship with God, self, others, and the whole of creation, and a process of giving and receiving life ensues. We accept that such radical relationship is the only way to wholeness and life. "Radical" means more than our common usage of "extreme;" it signifies getting to the roots or to something more basic or essential. It means a return to God and to the harmony and goodness of the creation as conceived by the love and life of God. It means walking in the garden with God in the cool of the evening, as we would an old friend. It means sharing a loaf of bread and a plate of fish that feed the world, so that no one goes to bed hungry or wakes up to find the cupboard bare. It means having and appreciating only what we need, rather than being bound by an endless insatiable thirst for things.

Indeed, the reality of God is an almost incomprehensible condition of mutuality, connectedness, and unity in the midst of abundant diversity. The radically relational reality of God is present within the web of creation where all things are connected and woven together by the hand of grace. Thus, we become our truest selves, not by defining ourselves apart from others, not in continuity with the societal forces that urge us to stumble along tempting but illusory paths to wholeness, not by eliminating any sense of our self, but through the transformative grace of God as it incorporates us into radically relational existence and expresses the fullness of God's love. No doubt, the message of identity in Christ is offensive or laughable to those who pursue individualism, power, success, and winning. It is unthinkable for those who wish to deny themselves to the point of virtual nonexistence. The Christ character confronts and threatens to unmask the illusory standards of society, whether those standards come cloaked in the language of faith or unabashedly ridicule the way of grace. When Jesus tells us to deny ourselves, he immediately adds, "and follow me." We can hear him say, "Let the Christ character flourish in you and make you fully human."

When we open ourselves to the revolutionary power of God's grace—putting aside our need to be first, best, most, least, or lowest—the Christ character takes shape within us and begins to overflow into the world. This outpouring of grace through us as the body of Christ in the world is what we are calling Godbearing. In today's world, much of our language of faith focuses either on morality-centered pronouncements or intellectually and emotionally satisfying expressions. Often such rhetoric seems to dominate the landscape of life in the United States. Today, everything from the coffee cups inscribed with inspirational slogans to the highest levels of government seems to speak of Christian faith. Of course, there is a level of superficiality to this God-talk, as it does not really attend to the brokenness of human life. Instead, it produces false hopes and subtly distracts us from the way of Christ in the world. Sometimes it exacerbates our brokenness—for example, when governments use the name of God to justify launching preemptive wars when no threat actually exists. Sometimes we convince ourselves that God really wants us to have a bigger house and super-sized SUV—a message proclaimed by so many "false apostles" of our age. Rather than honoring God, we use God to justify our own loveless plans. This sort of manipulation or seduction takes God's name in vain by suggesting we are following God when, in fact, we are pursuing our own schemes and dreams.

But when we open ourselves to participate in God, we enter into a spiritual reality that shakes the very structures of existence and reveals the brokenness of our lives and world. We want to "travel light" as Jesus urged, rather than spending a lifetime laying up treasures on earth. We become like the Christian recording artist who decided to keep what an average person earns each year and to give away all the rest of his income. A deep and pervasive relationality begins to take shape within us and, through us, in the world. The language of Godbearing expresses openness, otherness, service, restoration, and mutuality. It points toward grace-filled agency that stirs up and deepens radical relationship in the world. It emphasizes love and downplays judgment, leaving the determination of "winning" and "losing," right and wrong to the wisdom of God. It is the sweet and innocent love of a child that simply seeks the other without evaluating worthiness or gain. Judgment, winning, rightness, and similar concepts are comparatives in which we feel compelled to demonstrate our superiority. Humbleness, sacrifice, and suffering can also lead to comparatives that reinforce inferiority and subservience. But love has a simple confidence that need not assert itself in the comparative, as comparisons generally provide evidence of our brokenness. The love that does not insist upon its own way, even when rising up in prophetic boldness, models wholeness and resists the language of comparatives or superlatives. It remains unwavering in its wholeness, a reality that we are hard pressed to grasp in the midst of the brokenness of existence. This primacy of love, which finds its source and goal in God, embraces the whole of the created order and seeks its flourishing. It recognizes that when one atom of existence suffers, the God who is love seeks its renewal. The fullness of love in the world requires our participation as the body of Christ, for we who open ourselves to the radicality of love become the physical presence and tangible agents of God at work in the world. Through Godbearing we make known and make real the healing, transforming, life-giving and -receiving love of God in Christ in the Holy Spirit.

For many of us, a retreat apart from daily activities in the peaceful beauty of nature reminds us of the reality of God. For a moment, we are able to hear and see and smell the glory and presence of God. For others, an electrifying experience of the raw power of the Holy Spirit is a reminder of the reality of God breaking into existence. We feel a lightning bolt of grace surging through us. When these extraordinary experiences strike us, in a sudden moment of inspiration we are emboldened to simplify our lives, to seek a deeper connection with others, to find ways to serve those in need, to respect and honor the earth as our home. We simply and utterly are grasped by the knowledge that God IS. We know that we are God's. We feel that we are loved ultimately. And we vow to live differently from that day forward.

But upon returning to our ordinary lives, we find ourselves drawn back into the ways that turn us inward, scatter our awareness of God, and lead us back into brokenness. We become obsessed once again with comparatives and superlatives. The moment we drive onto the highway toward home and begin to wrestle with the traffic, we are hurled against the hardness and coldness of our world, jockeying for position. In order to maintain a sense of relationship with God, self, others, and creation, we need something more than the occasionally exhilarating or deeply peaceful brush with divinity. A moment's affective experience or intellectual insight is no substitute for the long, arduous, and disciplined journey of growing into the Christ character and overflowing into the world with God's love. We have to dig much deeper to get to the roots and to realize the radical relationality of God.

Thus, as we seek to enter into this journey, we find ourselves turning to the manna that God has provided in this wilderness of our lives in order to nourish our spirits and to find our way home: the scriptures, the sacred writings of the faith where we may discover ourselves and the meaning of life in God. The Bible is not a rule book that provides the dos and don'ts for the life of faith; rather, it is a travel guide that helps us to find our bearings in a new country and to understand the culture, customs, history, and reality of this new life in God. When we enter into the biblical narrative, the God-story, we begin to embrace the pattern of Godbearing and to embody Jesus' call to follow, to go deeper into the life he offers, the life of radical relationship.

THE WITNESSES OF SCRIPTURE

In the previous chapter, we argued that the term evangelism has ceased to be meaningful and should be reconceived in terms of God's revelation or self-disclosure. The revelation of the gospel in and through Jesus Christ enables us to grasp more clearly the nature of God, the fullness of humanity, and the reality of radical relationship. Yet, because our journey is to become fully human as we are created to be, rather than to become Jesus or God or an angelic spirit floating through the heavens, the gospel speaks to us about how to live in relationship to God, self, others, and the whole of creation in the midst of a difficult, messy, and earthy world. When the Christ character takes shape within us, it cannot help but overflow into the world. It is Rosa Parks's civil disobedience, quietly refusing to give up her seat on the bus and sparking a revolution of justice and human flourishing. It is the Catholic priest Bartolomé de Las Casas turning away from "civilizing" the indigenous peoples of South America to become their advocate and friend. It is the woman who begins a domestic abuse shelter in a small town in Iowa or the accountant who learns Spanish in order to provide free financial planning and tax preparation to the disadvantaged in El Paso. These are ordinary people whose lives become extraordinary through their openness to God. The overflowing or overabundance of grace is what we are calling the Christian practice of Godbearing. Jesus of Nazareth who is the Christ, who is the content of the gospel message, is the prototypical Godbearer and the basis for reawakening us to the ways of God in the world.

Godbearing, as the fruit of the Spirit blossoming within us, points us toward a threefold orientation or attitude toward life: 1) *bearing God* or bearing the renewed image of God within, 2) *bearing witness* or bearing faithful witness to God, and 3) *bearing suffering* or bearing with Christ the world's suffering. To be a follower of Christ means that we reorient or redirect our lives to be agents of life and love. We become planters of seeds and sowers of healing and wholeness. We become signs of transformative justice and grace in the brokenness that surrounds us. We become the quiet strength that refuses to let God's way be denied or diminished. We are urged by grace to be the glue binding what is broken, the balm salving what is raw, the sunlight warming and illuminating what is cold and cloudy—just as others are these same gifts to and for us.

In this chapter, our understanding of this orientation or pattern of Godbearing unfolds through the witnesses to Jesus of Nazareth who is the Christ, the One who brings the possibility of radical relationship into the world. Yet, because we are not and cannot become God, we must also turn to those who, though human, have opened their lives to being formed into the Christ character and enabled to be Godbearers in the world. Thus, in chapter 4 we will consider three Godbearers in the God-story: the traditional Godbearer, *Theotokos*, Mary the mother of Jesus; Mary Magadelene, who is sometimes called "the apostle to the apostles"; and the apostle Paul, whose "conversion" experience has been considered a model of renewed life through encounter with Christ. In the scriptural witnesses, we begin to recognize how the Christ character taking shape within us by grace enables the practice of Godbearing in the world to emerge. We are formed into community, straining toward wholeness, participating in Christ's work of weaving together the cosmos into the harmonious, flourishing reality intended by God.

The Varied Voices of Scripture

As we turn to the scriptural witnesses to develop our understanding of the identity of Jesus Christ, we are faced with the complexity of articulating the good news or God-story in a few pages. Whole books have been written on the subject without arriving at a definitive conclusion about the fullness of who Jesus Christ was and is and will be. The meaning of the biblical witnesses cannot be reduced to any one concise portrait, as Albert Schweitzer demonstrated decades ago in examining the so-called "Quest of the Historical Jesus." Schweitzer concluded that most investigators undertaking this quest discovered a Jesus who looked remarkably like themselves. While we do see ourselves in the living Christ, at the same time, we should note how significantly different he is from each of us. He is fully human; we are not yet. He is fully divine; we can never be. God in Christ in the Holy Spirit shares in the life of each human being, even as the triune God remains utterly distinct from us. With this tension in mind, we realize that we are called to enter into the fullness of our humanity, but we are not called to become Jesus. In other words, each of us is called to become the person who we were created to be by God. Yet, in order to understand what it means to be fully human, we need the revelation of God in Jesus of Nazareth to guide us and to illuminate our path. Who is Jesus Christ and how is this One, who is like us yet radically distinct from us, the content of the good news that leads us toward human flourishing?

Interpreting Jesus Yesterday and Today

One problem we encounter at this point, of course, is that who Jesus Christ is cannot be separated from who we today and interpreters throughout history understand him to be. In response to the question, "Who do you say that I am?" Harold Recinos notes that "the church has answered that Jesus is the Savior, the Son of God, a champion of nonviolence, the Lamb of God, brother, prophet, liberator, political revolutionary, Black Messiah, superstar, teacher, mystic Christ, Sophia, Prince of Peace, Consoler, unemployed laborer, an indigent, or social martyr."[1] We picture Jesus as the bloodied, sorrowful man of Mel Gibson's *The Passion of the Christ,* as the baby in the manger during our Christmas pageants, and as the victorious king riding down to earth on a cloud as the trumpet's blare announces the second coming. These are all, of course, metaphors and imaginative renderings rather than documentary evidence. Indeed, artwork from around the world depicts Jesus in vastly different and remarkably insightful ways.

This diversity of representations should not surprise us given that the scriptural witnesses themselves do not speak univocally, but with varying perspectives, emphases, and concerns. Among the gospels, for example, the differences "include emphases, selection, and order of incidents. There are variations in the ways the same incidents are described, and in the forms of the same sayings, the kinds of material favored, and the specific literary aims and plan of each author."[2] The Bible thus offers us layers of meaning and a richness of vision beyond any one person's ability to know and articulate fully. We begin to recognize that only the interplay of voices and perspectives of the New Testament woven together within the fabric of the Hebrew scriptures can begin to express the fullness of this One who is the heart of the Christian faith and the gospel message.

With the various voices giving shape to our visions of Jesus, we begin to grasp that the gospel is, at its very core, communal. It is only in the sharing of perspectives and interplay of voices that the fullest understanding of the One God among us begins to find faithful expression. Having a "God's eye" view of Jesus and the reality of God is humanly impossible on the individual level, and if we seek to draw nearer to the fullness of God, then we need the community to expand our horizons. This process is not unlike viewing a drawing of a vase that, when approached from different perspectives, can appear as a duck or the head of a person. At times, we can only reorient our vision when someone else points us toward the other perspective. The content of the gospel message is indeed inherently communal, for the messenger announces the news of restoration and flourishing to all, whether or not we hear or accept the report. The good news is not good news because of any human quality or action; it is so by the grace of God. But when we enter into and participate in this message, when we believe in God in Christ in the Holy Spirit taking shape in the world, we find ourselves already existing within this perplexing relationship or community we call the body of Christ. Those who claim they can believe in Christ and worship in their own way apart from others have failed to grasp the heart of the message, which, in a sense, announces that we are part of something much larger than ourselves. It is antithetical to believe in the triune God and to reject the community of God's people or the fullness of God's creation.

Moreover, when we consider that readers of the Bible, as well as the writers, are located in a wide range of historical and cultural settings, the complexity of the scriptural witnesses is multiplied. Because the Bible is a living Word, because the words we read are intimately related to the way and life of God, the content remains a dynamic process. It takes shape and exudes power in the reading and the hearing of the Word. We should think of our interaction with the Word of scripture as a relationship in its own right. The Bible as sacred scripture has a transformative power, presence, and meaning in the moment in which it is encountered and entered into. The scriptures possess a life-changing potential. When we sing, "I once was lost but now am found," we acknowledge that we were found by Amazing Grace rather than making our own way out of the wilderness. We have been drawn in by grace and find ourselves in a radically new relationship with God and the whole of God's creation. The scriptures invite us into this relationship; they do not simply invite us to enjoy a story. Stories end, but relationships continue to exist in multiple ways even beyond physical presence.

Yet, even after we are drawn into the radical relationality of grace, we remain human and subject to the frailties and imperfections of our creatureliness. R. S. Sugirtharajah has written, "As long as there are texts and readers, reading will be a consciously manufactured activity. Texts are malleable and readers are manipulative."[3] No doubt some will take offense at the charge of "manipulation," but Sugirtharajah confronts us with the sometimes uncomfortable truth that the "gospel" is and has been subject to use, misuse, and abuse through the centuries. We cannot remain blind to how the texts often function in the hands and desires of human beings. At the same time, Sugirtharajah also suggests to us that the "truth" of the gospel is not as immediately obvious and straightforward as many readers and proclaimers would lead us to think. The scriptures do not appear to us as a series of mathematical equations or natural laws that can be written and taught in simple sentences or "proven" to be valid through scientific means. We cannot fit all the pieces neatly together like a jigsaw puzzle to display the finished portrait of God and God's reign. Nor should we accept without question the teachings of a church or a pastor, as they too remain riddled with the human condition of brokenness and subject to the limits of finitude. Instead, we place ourselves before a living, breathing Word, sensitive to our proclivity to manipulate the Word and open to encounter anew even the most familiar texts. We approach the Word, hoping that we might be found by Grace, desiring to enter into the relationship offered. Although reading the Bible remains subject to the problematic nature of human activity and human error, it is also rife with possibilities for newness and growth.

Entering into the scriptures is thus a risky business, for misunderstanding is our lot in this world no matter how emphatically or authoritatively we present the meaning. It is also risky because we may hear the demand to change our ways and travel in a different direction. It is risky because we are called to live in the messiness of community—a reality that remains under the conditions of existence even as we enter into relationship with God and one another. Clearly, if the first followers of Jesus did not understand perfectly his message, we should refrain from expecting to achieve better results at a distance of two thousand years. If the first disciples were called to leave behind all manner of things, we should expect to hear, at times, a call to let go of one thing or another that keeps us from being open to participate more fully in life from God. If the earliest disciples sometimes found themselves in conflict with one another, we should expect to encounter similar difficulties. Nevertheless, despite the thorns and brambles that block our easy passage, the scriptures invite us into conversation and ask us to enter into the God-story. More important, they invite us to be shaped by the God-story and to reorient our lives through its message.

WITNESSING JESUS AS GODBEARER

Revealing the Fullness of Humanity

In his lectures on Christology, Dietrich Bonhoeffer once suggested that when we pose the question to Jesus, "Who are you?" Jesus responds, "Who are *you* to ask who am I?"[4] To ask after Jesus is to be confronted with relationship, relationship between God and humanity, among human beings, and even between readers and hearers and sacred texts in the mysterious process by which God is present through the Word. When we read the Bible, we are urged to open ourselves to relationship.

The heights and depths of the gospel are navigated neither by isolating the historical realities of Jesus of Nazareth nor by simply repeating his eschatological proclamation. While both the past and future aspects are necessary to grasping and living the gospel, the heart of the message is located in the present. As Augustine noted in his *Confessions*, all we really have is the present of the past, the present of the present, and the present of the future. Life demands our attentiveness in each moment, and to dwell excessively in either the past or the future is a sign of dis-ease. In Jesus of Nazareth who is the Christ, we discover what it means to be fully human and to open ourselves to the possibility of transformation in the present. Contemplating the existence of the Word become flesh enables us to discern the content of the gospel message, the good news that re-orients us toward what it means to be fully human. The gospel message, the life story of Jesus, directs us toward a new identity.

Jesus of Nazareth who is the Christ, the Messiah, is the prototypical Godbearer. From the outset, it is crucial to emphasize the fundamental and qualitative distinction that exists between this One who is the Messiah and those of us who seek to pattern our lives on the gospel: Jesus is the Christ, the one who brings life, and we are the recipients and sharers of his life-giving past, present, and future. Like the Roman soldier at the cross in Matthew 27:54, when we are shaken by the earthquake that is the reality of God, we cry out in awe: "Surely this one was God's Son!" To consider the identity of Jesus is to recognize both who we are and who we are not. It is to accept the possibilities for human existence that are found in following God in the world, choosing the way that leads to the flourishing of the whole of creation. It is also to accept that our journey is not to become God or Jesus Christ or some disembodied version of the Holy Spirit, but to enter into relationship with and through God in Christ in the Holy Spirit. Yet radical relationship with God, self, others, and all of creation is unlike any relationship we have known or experienced in the world with its pervasive condition of brokenness.

In the scriptural witnesses to Jesus we find a life-centered discourse; we are urged to open ourselves to life in the midst of death. We are like Ezekiel's dry bones as God breathes new cells and sinews into our scattered, broken fragments (Ezek. 37). Christians have long held that God came into the world in order that we might have life abundantly. In Jesus of Nazareth who is the Christ, the fullness of life through the embodiment of life-giving and life-receiving relationships becomes a real possibility. When we read the words of John 14:5–8 in this light, the significance of Jesus Christ comes into sharper focus. Thomas asks Jesus how we can know the way to where Jesus is going, and Jesus responds, "I am the way, and the truth, and the life. No one comes to the Father except through me." Traditionally, these words have been interpreted in an exclusionary sense; namely, that there is no way to life but through the Jesus named and proclaimed by Christians. Yet, the point of this passage is that of relationship: only those who are in radical relationship to God as revealed to us in and through Jesus of Nazareth who is the Christ, who is the One bringing restored relationship to humanity, can find the fullness of life. There is no way to abundant life without choosing to enter into the radically relational reality of God. Many times we have heard stories of missionaries who visited a place where Christians had never before been and, upon speaking about his or her faith, heard the indigenous person reply: "I've always known Jesus; I just didn't know his name." The mystery of the Way always exceeds our human grasp.

From the Christian perspective, the offer of radical relationship with God and creation is extended to all persons without qualification, but we must choose to participate, to accept the gift, to live in relationship with God and God's creation. Often Christians will emphasize the confession of Jesus as Savior as the key and sole requirement to eternal life; yet, if knowing Jesus and going his way are explored with care, we find that faith, the acceptance of God's way, is but the first stage of the relationship. It is not enough simply to believe in Jesus. When we believe, we become acquainted with God, but have not begun to grow into the fullness of the relationship that is revealed by God in Jesus Christ and through the Holy Spirit. To focus on confession alone is akin to marrying someone on the first date: we have hardly begun to know the other, let alone grasp who we are together.

As we explore the content of the God-story, the good news in and of Jesus Christ, in the following pages, we acknowledge that what is perfectly present in Jesus does not correspond directly to the embodiment of these characteristics in us. As human beings, as finite creatures, we always fall short of the fullness of our humanity in this life. Yet, we are able to enter into the ongoing process of reorientation toward the depths of life, as we allow the Christ character to take shape within us and overflow into the world as Godbearing. Godbearing in the world begins in and with this One. The radical relationship expressed as Godbearing consists of three distinct orientations or attitudes that are revealed in the life of Jesus: 1) bearing God within, 2) bearing faithful witness to God, and 3) bearing the suffering of others.

Bearing God Within

The witnesses to Jesus of Nazareth who is the Christ emphasize that Jesus bears the fullness of God within himself. In the beginning of the good news in and of Jesus Christ, we find the message of God with us in the infant born in Bethlehem. Wise men and shepherds pay homage to him; an earthly king is so utterly threatened by him that he lashes out against all children under the age of two, hoping to destroy this One (Matt. 2:16). Weeks later, when Jesus is brought by his parents to the temple, people again notice the fullness of God within him. We hear the voices of Simeon and Anna proclaiming him as the long-awaited Messiah. John the Baptist resists when Jesus presents himself to be baptized, acknowledging that Jesus is a greater bearer of God. Throughout his ministry, Jesus reveals the presence and power of God in his words and deeds, which causes people of diverse backgrounds and positions to declare his unusual authority. An example is the Samaritan woman in John 4:29 who, overwhelmed by her encounter with Jesus at the well, runs into the village and declares, "Come and see a man who told me everything I have ever done! He cannot be the Messiah, can he?" In the crucifixion scene of Matthew, we hear the Roman centurion, rocked by the earthquake, exclaim, "Truly this man was God's Son" (Matt. 27:54). Even the demon in the man with the unclean spirit cries out, "I know who you are, the Holy One of God" (Luke 4:34). Finally, in the transfiguration and, especially, the resurrection of Jesus, the gospels attest to the life-giving reality of God that Jesus bears within himself. Jesus of Nazareth who is the Christ is, as the tradition attests, fully divine.

Yet, in the midst of the many pronouncements of Jesus' authority and his identity in God, Jesus of Nazareth demonstrates a desire to continually renew and deepen his relationship with God. Matthew, for example, tells us that after feeding the five thousand, Jesus sent his disciples on ahead and "he went up the mountain by himself to pray" (14:23). In John, we find Jesus engaged in intercessory prayer on behalf of his disciples, modeling relationship with God and others (17:1–26). It is not enough for him to be blessed or approved by God; it is not enough for Jesus to declare his utter faith in God alone, as he does in the wilderness when tempted by the devil. When we are privy to Jesus in prayer or encounter the moments when he "goes apart" for an hour or a day to be alone in solitude, we witness Jesus entering into the depths that facilitate and enliven radical relationship. He also demonstrates to us that relationship with God—like any relationship—takes time, conversation, intimacy, and presence with the beloved. More importantly, in these instances we find Jesus placing himself in a receptive attitude, open to receive from God the gifts of relationship, life, love, and restoration.

Of course, we encounter a mystery when trying to make sense of how Jesus can be fully divine yet in relationship to God. How can Jesus, who is God, be in relationship to God? This logical conundrum can be answered from two perspectives. First, we must recognize that there is a relationship within God's self, what we generally refer to as the immanent or essential trinity, which cannot be contemplated from the human perspective, although theologians such as Augustine have attempted to describe the inner relationship of God in three persons. Nevertheless, the depths of the divine elude our grasp. In many ways, this comes as little surprise to us. We accept that in Jesus Christ we glimpse the definitive or fullest revelation of God, but not the fullness of the divine. God does not and cannot reveal the fullness of divinity to us, for we remain finite creatures incapable of the infinite. Yet, at the same time, we need only look at our own spouse, partner, or friend of twenty or forty years to realize that we do not fully grasp the inner workings of another human being. Indeed, we often do not even comprehend our own actions and inactions, as Paul so aptly described in Romans 7:15. Little wonder that we find the Trinity such an impenetrable mystery, despite those who, at times, attempt to reduce God to a series of moral pronouncements and stultified images, who seek to reduce the mystery of God to a very human representation with finite boundaries and specific characteristics that, inevitably, provide a level of comfort for the person who insists upon such reductionism.

From a second perspective, this paradox of Jesus as fully divine, yet in relationship to God is a model for what it means to be in right relationship with oneself. Here we can return to Paul in Romans 7 and his plea to be freed from the perplexities of seeking to live out of his own resources. Inevitably, when we try to build ourselves up or give ourselves away, we fall short of our full humanity. Perhaps this is one reason why we, in our contemporary context, are constantly tempted to pursue the bigger, better, or more exhilarating desire: if the fulfillment of becoming who we think we should be lies always just beyond our reach, then we need not face the fact that we do not really know ourselves. In Jesus of Nazareth we are shown that if we wish to know who we are and to be rightly related to our self, if we hope to find integrity and balance in our existence, if we wish to embrace the fullness of our humanity, then it must be done in relationship to God, who is the source of all right relationship. In a sense, the witnesses to Jesus Christ point to this radical relationship within Jesus himself. The phrase of the Great Commandment in which we are commanded to love our neighbor as our self is thus illuminated. To love ourselves, we must be in right relationship to the whole of our being—body, spirit, mind, and emotions—and this harmony is possible only by means of our openness to grace. To bear God within is to find ourselves in the midst of radical relationship not only to God, but also to ourselves—though as we will discover later in this chapter, for human beings, bearing God within means bearing the image of God within—an image renewed and more sharply delineated over the course of a lifetime as we remain open to ongoing relationship with God.

Bearing God to Others

With the first attitude of Godbearing in place—that is, the bearing of God within—we can turn to the second orientation seen in the life of Jesus of Nazareth who is the Christ: bearing God to others. In this sense, relationship with God leads Jesus to bear faithful witness to the one God revealed in the scriptures. The resurrected Christ proclaims a new way, which overcomes the death-dealing desires of the world that is threatened by the words, ways, and deeds of Jesus of Nazareth. We can suggest that Jesus bears faithful witness to God or points to the reality and radical relationality of God. It is important to keep in mind, however, that we should view the life of Jesus as an integral whole, in which his words and deeds flow from the rightly related person. This wholeness places before us the perspective best articulated by the Letter of James which indicates, better than most, that faith and works, words and deeds, thoughts and actions must flow from the same fountain. The life that Jesus as the prototypical Godbearer reveals to us is a life in which the whole of our existence glorifies God. His life points us toward dialogue, giving and receiving life, and embodying the witness we bear.

The Centrality of Dialogue

As a rabbi, Jesus is known by his teaching. Although we point to the "Sermon" on the Mount as an example of Jesus' preaching, the message he articulates is shared primarily through the venue of teaching, whether teaching among crowds or speaking to one or two persons. This mode of communication is significant because it suggests that we, too, proclaim the good news whenever we share the God-story with one or more persons. We can all be "teachers" in this sense of sharing the good news. In Jesus' many didactic moments, we are given a glimpse of the centrality of dialogue to the life of faith and of the basic contours of the life-giving discourse that he embodies.

First, we are struck by the dialogical nature of Jesus' teaching. Although his teachings are authoritative because he alone knows the fullness of God and the fullness of humanity, Jesus nonetheless engages in give-and-take exchanges. The instances in the gospels in which the teaching moment is a moment of dialogue and conversation are too numerous to recount, though a few examples will illustrate this point. First, Jesus is often in dialogue with his disciples, such as when he asks them, "Who do people say that I am?" (Mark 8:27). It is a Socratic method in which he knows the answer but hopes to help the disciples arrive at sound conclusions through conversation. Beyond his inner circle, he engages in conversations with a variety of people—from those who simply approach with a question, such as the man in Mark 10:17 who runs up and asks, "Good Teacher, what must I do to inherit eternal life?" to "outsiders," such as the woman at the well in John 4 or the Roman Centurion in Matthew 8:5, and even to the religious leaders of his day, such as Nicodemus in John's gospel or the religious authorities in Luke 20 who question Jesus' authority.

Although this manner of teaching is consistent with the role of a rabbi in first-century Palestine, it is significant to recognize that Jesus often teaches by way of dialogue and enables others to arrive at their own conclusions. We are all familiar with contemporary churches and church leaders who teach by pronouncement and reject any form of questioning or inquiry. Such monological teaching is common. Yet, when Jesus bears God to others, his words often draw the questioner into a conversation, in which he listens as well as offers answers. In this sense, Jesus of Nazareth recognizes that real relationship involves dialogue. We know this to be true with our children; early on they begin to ask us questions about the sky's blueness and the wagging tail of the dog. Once they begin a conversation, they will often continue to ask questions until they are satisfied or we are stumped by the query and simply sit together before the mystery. Real relationship respects the God-given gifts of human free will and mutuality that are the basis of all true relationship. To bear God to others is not to insist upon our own way, but to offer relationship to all through the intimacy of conversation in which we both give and receive. Teaching is thus a form of openness to enter into relationship with any and all as we maintain Jesus of Nazareth as our model and guide. To be a faithful disciple is to be in conversation with God and others and to recognize that the conversation never comes to closure.

The Life-Giving and -Receiving Message

In his dialogical teaching, Jesus also reveals the contours of the life-centered message of the God-story. Three well-known gospel passages will enable us to sketch the basic parameters of the life-transforming possibilities present in his teaching: first, the Sermon on the Mount in Matthew 5, second, the question, "What must I do to inherit eternal life?" as posed in the Gospel of Luke, and third, John 3:16. Of course, these texts are among those most frequently used to present basic teachings of the Christian faith, which indicates their traditional importance in conveying the good news. At the same time, although these three passages enable us to wrestle with the content of the message that is Jesus Christ, it remains impossible to describe the entirety of his message in a few brief pages and in one historical and cultural moment.

The Sermon on the Mount One of the most extensive of Jesus' teaching moments found in the gospels is the Sermon on the Mount. It provides us with an initial glimpse of the life-centered heart of the good news revealed in Jesus of Nazareth who is the Christ. This lengthy passage, which extends from Matthew chapter 5 through chapter 7, is centered on a basic understanding of the radical relationality that Jesus embodies. It opens with the Beatitudes, which provide a sense of what relationship with God entails and what it means to be blessed by God. We are not told that faith in God in Christ in the Holy Spirit will provide us with a lifetime supply of worldly treasures and pleasures, but we are given a glimpse of what human flourishing, blessedness, or happiness means in the eyes of God. Being blessed by God entails comfort for those who mourn, inheritance for those who are meek, righteousness for those who seek it, mercy for the merciful, seeing God face-to-face for the pure in heart, adoption as God's children for those who pursue peace. These are not so much present realities as they are promises, for the Beatitudes close with a call to perseverance in the way of faith, even when the world ridicules or despises the choice to follow Christ. Our relationship with God does not bring us wealth, individual success, or the power to dominate others. It does not place us into a position that those enamored with the world's ways will find enviable. In other words, Jesus begins his sermon by clarifying how different the reign of God really is from the world's brokenness. If we truly desire to follow God's way, it is not possible to cling to the world's version of happiness and human flourishing.

Then, in his references to being the salt of the earth (5:13) and the light of the world (5:14), Jesus begins to illuminate the meaning of relationship. Having drawn a line between those who seek God's reign and those enamored by worldly gain, he expresses how the reign of God begins to breech the barriers the world constructs to keep God's way at bay. People of faith, in radical relationship to God, are called to be flavorful salt and a shining light; we are called to live in a way that reflects and seasons what it means to be blessed by God. To proclaim that one's financial portfolio, Ferrari, fame, or first-place finish is the blessing of God is to hold a mirror up to the world's standards rather than to stir up the flame of God's love. When we drink deeply of the world's intoxicating ways, we cannot taste and see that God is good (Psa. 34:8) and find it impossible to offer others the flavor of God's goodness. But when we allow ourselves to be shaped by God's love and reign, others will see the reflection of God and, perhaps, be drawn toward that light and want to taste and see for themselves. Clearly, bearing faithful witness to others is a matter of pointing with our whole being toward the glory of God in the midst of radical relationship.

Yet, beyond this message that we should be agents of God's grace, drawing others to the path that leads to the fullness of life, we find that Jesus considers our attitude toward others as an expression of our radical relationship to God or lack thereof (Matt. 5:17–48). He denounces anger toward others and demands reconciliation, condemns not only adultery but even the thoughts or feelings that would desire to enter into such brokenness, insists that retaliation is the way of the world and going the extra mile is the way of relationship. Indeed, in stark contrast to societal standards, Jesus commands love for enemies, which stands as, perhaps, the most extreme sign of radical relationship. In today's terms, Jesus would ask U.S. Christians if we are willing to love Al Qaeda and the Taliban, as well as our political opponents. God's radically relational love seeks the flourishing of all, and those who follow God's way are required to enter fully into that reality, which runs counter to much of what society and so-called "common sense" would have us believe and do.

Beginning in Matthew 6 and continuing through chapter 7, Jesus places before his hearers a vision of the radically relational self.

In what does the integrity or wholeness of a human being consist? First, Jesus teaches about the integrity of our worship life, suggesting that giving alms, praying, or fasting should not be done in order to be seen by others. From a contemporary perspective, we sometimes seek to be better Christians, more pious, bigger givers. We paste Jesus bumper stickers on our cars and wear crosses around our necks. We volunteer at our church, but resent it when the pastor fails to acknowledge our contributions. But seeking some form of public approval is a sign that we are not in proper relationship to our self, and that we base our identity on the image or persona we convey to others and their approval or praise. We all know people who would rather look good than be good, who live by the motto, "Image is everything." But what lies beneath our masks, the intention of our hearts, is the surest measure of radical relationship—and measurable ultimately only by God in Christ in the Holy Spirit.

The contemporary emphasis on individualism is called into question when Jesus teaches about prayer. The prayer we call "the Lord's Prayer" in Matthew 6 begins by articulating a communal identity that points toward the radical relationality of those who have faith in God. Notably, it uses the first person plural: *Our* Father, give *us*, forgive *us*. Central to this relationality are three basic attitudes toward life: 1) seeking to act in accordance with God's will, 2) asking only for what we need each day rather than to fulfill our endless desires, and 3) giving and receiving forgiveness. In these three basic attitudes, the radical relationship among God, self, others, and the whole of creation is cultivated. To seek God's will is to choose relationship over individual advancement; to ask for only as much as we need is to respect both the earth's limited resources and the needs of others; and to give and receive forgiveness is to engage in the hard practice of reconciliation in large and small ways. As Archbishop Desmond Tutu reminds us, forgiveness and reconciliation require justice as well. Perhaps we repeat the Lord's Prayer too frequently to hear clearly the emphasis on finding our true identity within the midst of relationship, honoring the healthy giving and receiving that is essential to the heights and depths of God's own love.

The message of radical relationship that confronts individualism, consumerism, and imperialism is reinforced in the final verses of Matthew 6 and through the end of chapter 7. The desire for individual advancement and self-actualization is challenged by the Golden Rule, as it is impossible to aim to be or to have the most and the best in societal terms and to do unto others as we would have them do unto us. Indeed, when we ignore the Golden Rule and choose the way of comparatives and superlatives, we then begin to judge others; something that Jesus warns against in the strong language of hypocrisy. No one can serve two masters (6:24).

The desire for conspicuous and unrestrained consumption is soundly denounced by Jesus: "Do not store up for yourselves treasures on earth" (6:19). Again, he cautions, "Do not worry about your life, what you will eat or what you will drink, or about your body, what you will wear. Is life not more than food, and the body more than clothing?" (6:25). Of course, Jesus is not recommending extreme ascetic behavior, but rejecting the constant worry about material things, which can consume our thoughts and devour or sour our relationships. Nor is Jesus suggesting that those who have no nutritious food, no potable water, no clothing or shelter to protect them from the elements should not be concerned about them. Rather, in the context of his constant admonition to care for the widow, the orphan, and the stranger—those who have no visible means of support—it stands as a message against an inappropriately desirous relationship toward material goods. Enough is enough, Jesus says. "You cannot serve God and wealth" (6:24).

Finally, we can read these passages as calling into question the imperial desires that come with the accumulation of power. Jesus cautions against "false prophets" who are "inwardly ravenous wolves," wanting to devour everything in sight (7:15). "You will know them by their fruits," he admonishes (7:16). Are the fruits of their God-talk destruction of life and limb? Are the fruits of their actions "in God's name" those of gargantuan military budgets and the impoverishment of the lives of innocents? The teaching of Jesus then punctuates with two exclamation marks this distinction between those who hear or speak God's words and those who embody them. First, he warns that "Not everyone who says to me, 'Lord, Lord,' will enter the kingdom of heaven, but only the one who does the will of my Father in heaven" (7:21). He concludes this warning against self-deception by noting that many will claim to have done deeds of power in his name, but Jesus will not recognize them, for the deeds do not resemble those of the blessed who are peacemakers, merciful, and pure in heart.

Second, he ends his sermon with the clear command to do his words rather than simply to hear or speak them. It is a command to embody his words, to live our lives out of and through them. We do not find Jesus claiming: Blessed are the peacemakers who first drop billions of dollars of bombs and destroy cities and torture the enemy, send in no-bid contract corporations with political ties to rebuild at an enormous cost, and then proclaim a victory for democracy and freedom in the name of God. He forces us to ask: Do the ends justify the means? The Sermon on the Mount seems to cast this question into doubt, as it describes the desire for imperial power, to rule over others in the name of God, as a false prophecy: "On that day, many will say to me, 'Lord, Lord, did we not prophesy in your name, and do many deeds of power in your name . . . ?' Then I will declare to them, 'I never knew you; go away from me, you evildoers.'" (7:22–23). No one can serve two masters.

Luke and the Question of Inheriting Eternal Life Given the basic orientation presented in the Sermon on the Mount, the teachings in Luke 18:18–30 and 10:25–37 and John 3:16 come into sharper focus. The question of inheriting eternal life is posed by "a certain ruler" in Luke (or a rich young man in Matthew), who undoubtedly possesses some measure of power along with wealth (Luke 18:18). After pointing to the Ten Commandments, which are central to the reality of radical relationship, Jesus indicates that this man continues to be caught in the grip of riches. He leaves saddened by the idea of having to give away his earthly treasures and chooses to walk away rather than to follow Jesus. The person who bears faithful witness to God does not cling to earthly power, self-desire, or material goods, but is willing to leave all behind for the sake of the offered relationship. Clearly, to seek eternal life is to accept the way of radical relationship with God, self, others, and creation. But when we cling to the desires promoted and sustained by our society, we choose not to be in radical relationship. We prefer to live comfortable lives rather than to follow Jesus who has no place to lay his head and only one staff and tunic. But no one can serve two masters. There exists an either/or choice in a world of unlimited desires: Either we opt for the radical relationship that exists only in the reality of God or we opt for the world's brokenness, however we may name it. Life in God in Christ in the Holy Spirit is inescapably relational, such that if we choose God, we choose relationship with self, others, and the entire web of creation as central to life abundant and lasting. However, this does not mean we will embody perfectly such relationality in this life, which begs the question of eternal life in which radical relationality is realized in its fullness.

In Luke 10, the question, "What must I do to inherit eternal life?" is placed in the mouth of a lawyer "testing" Jesus, who responds with the Great Commandment to love God and to love your neighbor as yourself (10:27). When the lawyer continues the dialogue, asking: "And who is my neighbor?" Jesus offers the parable of the Good Samaritan in which the "outsider," the Samaritan passing by, shows compassion to the wounded man and generously pays his expenses. Yet, even more significant in the flow of the gospel is that this parable follows upon the heels of a significant passage related to bearing faithful witness to others: the mission of the seventy. What does the mission of the seventy tell us about bearing faithful witness to others? Several aspects of the text are particularly striking: those who are sent go in pairs, as two gathered together rather than as lone evangelists. They are commanded to carry as little as possible and to depend upon the hospitality of others; in other words, they are sent not only to give but also to receive, thus creating relationships that involve sharing and mutuality and, of course, humility. Then, when the seventy return, they exult over the power that they possessed in the course of their mission. Jesus cautions them not to take to heart the power and the authority, but rather to rejoice only in the grace of God and to give glory to God.

At times, we depend upon the hospitality of others to provide us with directions when we are lost in a strange city or to offer assisitance when we have a flat tire. To ask for help requires some measure of humility and willingness to be in relationship. Sometimes we are on the giving end of such exchanges, being the one who has the power to offer assistance. Either way, the moment of giving and receiving lingers with us long after the moment of sharing.

I remember many years ago being in the main train station in Seoul on a Korean holiday, utterly confused by the tens of thousands of people crowded together and my inability to speak or read the language. Standing with my ticket in hand, suitcase at my feet, unable to determine where to go to board my train, a middle-aged woman trotted over to me. Smiling, she looked at my ticket, grabbed my bag, and ran off into the crowd, signaling to me to follow. A minute or two later we arrived at a train platform, where she placed my bag on the ground and waved good-bye as she disappeared back into the throng of holiday travelers. As she vanished I could only yell after her: *Kamsamnida!* Thank you! It was a small act of relationship but remains in my memory as a glimmer of the living Christ among us.

John 3.16 Finally in John 3:16 we find ourselves confronted with the oft-quoted text: "For God so loved the world that he gave his only Son, so that everyone who believes in him may not perish but may have eternal life." What must we do to inherit eternal life? To answer this question, the verse should be placed into the larger context of John chapter 3. This chapter begins with Nicodemus's visit to Jesus under cover of darkness and their ensuing, albeit somewhat disconnected, dialogue. Central here is the claim that eternal life requires belief in the "Son of Man" and "the name of the only Son of God." Theologically, we encounter a significant point in this dialogue, as Jesus refers to himself in terms of both the Son of Man (3:13, 14) and Son of God (3:18), while using the phrase "his only Son" in verse 16. Since the phrase "son of" means "belonging to the family of" in the context of the Hebrew scriptures, we can read the Christological titles as "the One belonging to the family of Humanity" and "the One belonging to the family of God." Thus, when John quotes Jesus as saying that God "gave his only Son," we are confronted with a moment of radical relationality. With 3:16 sandwiched between the specific titles, John recalls the incarnation as the pivotal moment in which the radical relationship between God and humanity is bridged and provides the possibility of reconciliation to all. Thus, to believe in the name of the One who is both fully human and fully divine is to enter into radical relationship with God in Christ in the Holy Spirit. This pivotal point is reinforced at the conclusion of chapter 3 when John comments about the one who comes from above, where the language of "the Son" is used without the qualifiers "of Man" or "of God." Whoever believes in, has faith in, trusts in, and accepts the way of this call to relationship will find eternal life. Those who reject this radically relational reality will remain mired in the broken dreams and desires of individual existence.

When we ask about bearing faithful witness to God, Jesus points us toward the radical relationality he initiates and offers as the basis of life in its fullness. We are called to enter into dialogue and conversation as central to faithful testimony, thus suggesting we are to enter into relationships of giving and receiving, mutuality, and listening, rather than insisting upon our own way or condemning others who do not grasp the fullness of life that is offered. Even prophetic boldness should not be seen as primarily an act of condemnation, but rather as a call to return to God. Prophetic speech remains in dialogue with God and others. At the same time, the teaching of Jesus points toward radical relationship as basic to the good news. Radical relationship agrees to follow a different orientation in life, one that does not seek material wealth, individual success, or imperial power, but desires the mutuality and harmony that is fundamental to relationship. We are called to enter into this delicate balance of giving and receiving life, casting our nets out into deep relationships with God, others, and creation and pulling them back gently toward ourselves—and, for that matter, allowing ourselves to be pulled back into such relationship when we stray from it.

Embodying Radical Relationship

Bearing faithful witness to God involves not only our speech about this call to radical relationship, but also and especially embodying such relationality. This call to action, to embodiment, to being agents of God is also seen in Jesus of Nazareth. Jesus is, of course, known for his miracles. The healing stories presented in the gospels are numerous and demonstrate the restoration of radical relationship. When the Syrophoenician or Canaanite woman's daughter is restored to health, Jesus enables the integrity of the daughter to flourish, as well as her relationships with others. When the five thousand are fed by a few fish and loaves of bread with seven baskets left over, Jesus, the disciples, and the people gathered together nourish the flourishing of community. When the turbulent seas are calmed, Jesus restores harmony to the relationship between humanity and creation. Whatever the need presented to Jesus, it inevitably entails brokenness from God and others, from the integrity of the self, and even from a proper relationship with creation. Jesus restores the possibility of relationship, though each person must find his or her identity in Christ and allow himself or herself to become a Godbearer in the world. This point is significant because we cannot expect to perform the same level of miraculous acts as Jesus, but we can each see ourself as one who has been touched and transformed and who is commanded to continue in the way of God in Christ in the Holy Spirit in the world.

Bearing witness with our lives is certainly at the center of Matthew's discourse on the judgment of the nations in chapter 25. The flourishing of life is not found in the mere confession of the name of the One who belongs to God and to humanity; rather, it is found in continuing the witness of radical relationality in our daily and often ordinary existence. We are told to feed the hungry, to clothe the naked, to visit prisoners, to welcome the stranger among us, to care for those who are sick. Each of these things is a "miracle" in its own right, for when we facilitate these acts of mercy, we become agents of the radical relationality of God. We redistribute the earth's precious resources so that all may find life. We offer the gift of presence to those who are isolated and alone. We provide for the needs of those who cannot provide for themselves. In doing so, we enter into the reality of giving and receiving life as modeled and embodied by Jesus Christ.

When we enter into radical relationship with God, the Christ character takes shape within us and will overflow to others, not simply in the giving of alms, but more profoundly in the establishing of relationships that lead to flourishing. We are not called merely to write a check and mail it to a good charity, preserving the cancelled check as an income tax deduction. We are not asked simply to schedule a pickup of our discards to be distributed to the needy. We are not commanded to cheer the execution of a death row inmate. We are not called to conquer others so that we might impose a different way of life upon them. But we are commanded to facilitate the flourishing of abundant life in and through the mutuality and integrity of radical relationship. We are called to enter into relationship with our neighbor and the stranger in our midst. Perhaps it means volunteering to work with Meals on Wheels, delivering food and a friendly face to the homebound. Maybe we are to join with Sister Helen Prejean in fighting to eliminate the death penalty in the United States. Perhaps we are called to adopt the dog or cat that has been at our local pound for the longest time and to help our community set up a spaying and neutering clinic. Perhaps we are called to join a church that is ethnically diverse so that we might be transformed through the ongoing encounter with others and be a source of transformation in the days between Sundays. This represents resurrection: life emerges out of death-dealing situations. This is how we can proclaim Jesus of Nazareth becoming instruments of life, despite the ways of the world. Through faith in God in Christ in the Holy Spirit our lives can be fundamentally reoriented and reconfigured as weavers of the fabric of life and sowers of the seeds of flourishing.

Bearing the Suffering of Others

The third aspect or orientation of Godbearing is illuminated by our previous foray into Matthew 25. No matter how deeply we are able to enter into radical relationship by the grace of God, we are unable to relieve the world's suffering and reconcile the whole of creation. Even though we may visit the prisoner, we cannot free him or the countless others who are imprisoned. Though we may feed the hungry in our neighborhood, we cannot eliminate starvation across the face of the earth. Though we may clothe the naked, we cannot eliminate the international economic systems that rely upon cheap labor in developing countries and leave so many with mere pennies and desperately damaged environments. Though we may welcome the stranger who has fled a war-torn nation, we cannot stop the machinery of racial profiling in the name of preserving freedom and democracy. While it is not ours to bring the fullness of life to fruition, we are commanded to alleviate suffering whenever possible, as we participate in the transformation of the whole of creation. The principle of proximity prevails, and in our finitude we can only provide for those we encounter in concrete circumstances, as the Samaritan does along the road from Jerusalem to Jericho. What the Samaritan models is not an end to violence and pain, but the bearing of another's suffering in tangible ways. Yet, in this one historical and cultural moment, we glimpse and participate in the new creation, where death and suffering are no more.

When we recognize that, in our finitude, we cannot ameliorate all the suffering that exists throughout creation, we are led to bear with patient love the suffering of others, to stand with and beside them in their pain, heaviness, and brokenness. When we visit the hospital to sit with a coworker whose child is dying, we cannot heal the child. But our presence, our gift of food for the family, our calls and cards, and our expressions of caring can help them to bear the unbearable. When we speak out against the violence in Darfur or Congo, contacting our elected officials and demanding that the United States not turn a blind eye, we stand with those who suffer. We are called to speak and acknowledge the truth of our brokenness and to work toward reconciliation by the grace of God. This claim stems from the image of the crucifixion to which we must turn in order to grasp the meaning of bearing the suffering of others. Traditionally, Christians have proclaimed that it was God's plan that Jesus should suffer and die to reconcile us to God. Yet, to put forth the claim that it was God's will for Jesus to be the sacrifice that atones for our sins fails to acknowledge our complicity in Jesus' death on the cross two thousand years ago and even today. The claim that Christ died for the sins of humanity is cloaked in the language and theology of the Hebrew sacrificial system in which the high priest offered up a living piece of creation as a means of atonement. Thus, when we draw upon this imagery to explain the death of Jesus of Nazareth, we make two theological errors.

First, because we believe in one God expressed in three names, we make the illogical claim that God required a sacrifice of God's own self to appease God's wrath or that God took upon God's self the punishment that we deserved from God. Such atonement theories are problematic since they often portray God as requiring something from God to satisfy God. When we are honest with ourselves, we cannot pin all the blame for Jesus' death on God—heaven forbid—or on "those people" who sent Jesus to the cross. If the incarnation initiated the reconciliation of God and humanity in this one historical and cultural point, then we cannot argue that God required the death of God's very Self. In this case, human free will intervened. Threatened and exposed for who we really are, we demanded the death of Jesus rather than having to change and to reorient our lives toward God as God truly is rather than the God of our expectations and desires. Today, when we refuse the way of radical relationship, when we refuse to participate in the fullness and flourishing of life, metaphorically, we continue to put Jesus to death. We continue to reject his message of life and reorientation. We seek our own gain, often in the name of preserving the purity of the faith and the truth. If Jesus must undergo suffering and death, it is not because God wills it, but because God knows that humanity in its brokenness will demand crucifixion. Like the angry and threatened mob at the cross we cry out, "Crucify him!" As broken human beings, we are more inclined to judgment than to love, and judgment without love refuses to hear, engage, or be in dialogue with the other.

The second theological error is inherent in the notion of a sacrificial system, in which God demands death in order that relationship might be restored. Such belief contradicts the reality of a God who created and sustains life and seeks its flourishing. The idea that God would ask us to kill a bird, a goat, a lamb, or a human being in order that we might be in right relationship with God is deeply problematic when we take to heart the words and witness of the scriptures and of Jesus of Nazareth who is the Christ, who reveals to us the fullness of the divine and the human. The prophet Hosea reminds us that God declares, "I desire steadfast love and not sacrifice, the knowledge of God rather than burnt offerings" (6:6). Or as the psalmist reiterates, "For you have no delight in sacrifice; if I were to give a burnt offering, you would not be pleased. The sacrifice acceptable to God is a broken spirit; a broken and contrite heart" (Psalm 51:16–17). Jesus wept as he stood on the hill overlooking Jerusalem, grieved by the world's broken ways. When one atom of creation suffers, when one drop of blood is shed in hatred, when one teardrop falls in the depths of grief, God suffers, bleeds, and weeps. God calls us into radical relationship with every molecule of the created universe.

Although we must tread carefully upon our conception of the cross, what it reveals clearly is the willingness of God to bear our burdens, to allow us to exercise our free will, and to remain steadfastly in relationship to us. God will not sever the relationship, even in our ugliest moments; indeed, to do so would contradict the very nature of the God who is love and radical relationship. But we human beings can choose to destroy life, to uphold our ways as the absolute truth, to seek our own self-interests in the name of God. We can be the purveyors of the cross who seek to destroy the radical relationality and reconciliation in our midst, refusing to reorient our lives. We can buy a new Hummer, arguing that God wants us to have the finer things in life, while complaining about the foreign countries who are raising our gas prices. We can shield our child's eyes from the homeless man or woman on the street, teaching her that the homeless are to be feared and avoided. Or we can choose to follow the patient, peaceful, bold, and life-centered way of Jesus and to accept that radical relationship entails bearing the suffering of others. We can refuse to allow the world's brokenness to twist injustice and hatred into a façade of acceptable, even normative behavior in the name of God or religious principles. For example, we can choose to worship at a church in a poor neighborhood or with the homeless at the shelter downtown, knowing that God calls us to become open to others at a deeper level.

In a nuanced description of suffering, Dietrich Bonhoeffer argued that those who follow Christ participate in the sufferings of creation in a transformed and transforming manner. Rather than suffering simply at the hands and hearts of a broken world, suffering in Christ is about sharing in the burdens and weights that others carry. It is about giving and receiving—not only peacefulness and joy—but also the suffering and pain of others, which we take unto ourselves in the gift of relationship that helps them to bear that pain. To stand with and beside those who suffer is a form of God's radically relational presence. The image here is quite distinct from the one often witnessed in the televangelistic prayer of healing, in which the televangelist reaches out to send the power of God's Spirit through his hand into the pitiable person who has stumbled to the stage. It is an image of someone claiming God's power, towering over the wounded to dispense this power. It is an image of the televangelist as privileged purveyor of power not given to the ordinary person.

But the image that we find in Jesus of Nazareth is that of taking the pain onto himself, of receiving the suffering of another in order to lighten that person's load. It is not about setting himself "above" those who are broken, as somehow more privileged or superior. Instead, he enters into the suffering of the world. Jesus kneels to wash the dirty, smelly feet of his disciples, taking unto himself their world weariness. Jesus refuses to take up arms and destroy his enemies on behalf of the forces of good. Jesus offers to share our burdens when we find the world almost too heavy to bear. We might say that, rather than serving as a fire hose to extinguish the suffering as we pour out the Spirit of God, we are asked to be like a vacuum that draws the suffering inward to reduce that which is present to others. Backpackers understand this idea: when one person is hurting and can barely continue along the trail, others who are stronger will offer to take some of the load from that person's pack into theirs so that they all might continue the trek together. This is what it means to lay down one's life; it is a willingness to be in radical relationship and share in one another's pain and brokenness without expecting some form of tangible gain. We choose the way of suffering in order that radical relationship might continue to prevail against evil, hatred, and injustice. Though we cannot take away suffering and death, we can help others to bear it and even to break its grip on the surrounding society.

At this point one caution articulated well in feminist theologies bears reiterating. Since the 1960s when Valerie Saiving published her landmark article, feminists have argued that women have too often poured themselves out entirely for others.[5] Their sin, according to Saiving, is not that of pride as male theologians have portrayed through the ages, but the selflessness by which they pour themselves out completely in being for others. Although this position has since undergone considerable critique and modification, it remains a valuable insight for men and women alike who desire selflessness. Were this the way and the meaning of the cross, then Jesus would have endured the crucifixion without reference to the integrity of his person. If Jesus had displayed no self-concern he would not have cried out to God, "Why have you forsaken me?" (Mark 15:34). If Jesus had abandoned the integrity of his humanity, he would not have sought relationship with others in the Garden of Gethsemane, begging his friends, his followers to stay awake with him in his hour of suffering. Even Jesus of Nazareth understood that the healthy self cannot and will not endure alone the pain and suffering and the brokenness of the world. The radically relational self does not seek to give himself or herself away until nothing remains, but seeks to receive life as well as to give it.

In bearing the suffering of others, we realize that because life has been woven together by the finger of God, when one particle of creation suffers, the whole suffers. When one strand of DNA goes astray, the implications extend well beyond that unseen double helix. Moreover, in Jesus of Nazareth, the impulse toward inclusion, the respect for otherness, the recognition that we are all part of God's created earth become visible. The scriptures indicate that Jesus was open and available to everyone, but especially noteworthy is his attentiveness to those whom mainstream society was likely to ignore or marginalize. For example, in a culture where men were not particularly likely to welcome small children into their arms in public, particularly other people's children, Jesus invited them to sit with him. Jesus related to those who were foreigners or enemies to Israel, whether the Samaritan woman at the well with an indiscrete past (John 4), the Syrophoenician or Canaanite woman who would not be denied Jesus' healing power (Mark 7:24–30, Matt. 15:21–28), or the leper whose uncleanliness had isolated him from community (Luke 5:12–14). In responding to this wide variety of people, Jesus did not "heal" all the conditions that kept them from experiencing the fullness of life: non-Israelites were not reconciled to Israel, women still had lesser rights than men in the ancient world, and the eventuality of death would be the lot of every man, woman, and child he healed of some illness. Yet, when Jesus encountered injustice, exclusion, indifference, or hatred, he did what he could to ease the suffering and reestablish life-giving and receiving relationships. Bearing the suffering of others in order to participate in the giving and receiving of life in its fullness is central to the work of Godbearing that is revealed in Jesus of Nazareth. Thus, we are called to pick up our own crosses and enter into relationships that enable others to bear the burden of suffering and pain until Christ returns again to finish what began to take shape in Jesus of Nazareth.

In sum, the witnesses to Jesus of Nazareth who is the Christ provide us with a deep and broad understanding of the threefold orientation of Godbearing in the world: bearing God (or the image of God) within, bearing faithful witness to God in words and actions, and bearing the suffering of others. This threefold orientation to life encapsulates the basic God-story revealed in Jesus of Nazareth. In bearing God within we find the reality of incarnation at work. In bearing faithful witness to God we encounter the ministry and resurrection of Jesus. In bearing the suffering of others we see the crucifixion that continues to say "no!" to the death-dealing ways of our society. As we await the return of the One God who became enfleshed in the world, we who compose the body of Christ are called to the work of Godbearing in the world. Yet, we cannot be or offer the fullness of life that was present in Jesus of Nazareth who is the Christ. As such, it is essential to conceptualize the shape and context of Godbearing, this threefold orientation toward the giving and receiving of life, as it is embodied and expressed in followers of God in Christ in the Holy Spirit. For this purpose, in chapter 4, we will consider briefly three significant biblical figures (Mary, the mother of Jesus; Mary Magdalene; and Paul, the apostle to the Gentiles) and two historical Godbearers (Bartolomé de Las Casas and Rosa Parks). Their stories enable us to grasp more clearly what it means to express the gospel in our world today.

four FOLLOWING JESUS

In the previous chapter, the scriptural witnesses to Jesus of Nazareth revealed the threefold pattern of Godbearing: bearing God within, bearing faithful witness to God, and bearing with God the suffering of others. With this pattern in mind, we can now move beyond the prototypical and revelatory form found in Jesus and ask about Godbearing among his followers. Discipleship or following the way of Jesus means embodying Godbearing in the world. In this chapter, we examine briefly three scriptural and two historical figures who demonstrate the possibility of sharing in the Godbearing life to which Jesus Christ calls us. Our examination begins with Mary, the Mother of God; Mary Magdalene; the Apostle to the Apostles; and Paul, the Apostle to the Gentiles, then turns to the lives of Bartolomé de Las Casas and Rosa Parks. These figures enable us to expand our understanding of Godbearing. Through them, we begin to see how we, ourselves, might enter into the way of Godbearing in the world.

MARY, *THEOTOKOS,* GODBEARER

We all know Mary; at least, our images of Mary are rather straightforward. Mary is the sweet young girl sitting by the manger in Bethlehem. She is the distraught woman standing beside the cross who is "given" the beloved disciple as her son. She is the ornately painted saint, gilded in gold, holding the baby Jesus in her arms. We sing Christmas carols and plan pageants celebrating this innocently virginal mother or fiercely maternal virgin. But our images of Mary may arise more from two thousand years of interpretation by the church and less from the depths of Mary's life in God to which the scriptures bear witness. Indeed, for generations, biblical scholars and theologians have debated Mary's role in the God-story. Protestantism has often criticized the Marian devotion of the Roman Catholic and Orthodox traditions as extreme and unwarranted. Yet Protestants do little better, often relegating her to the nativity scenes that decorate our churches each Advent season, leaving her to stand as a voiceless clay figurine.

In recent years, feminists have criticized the traditional image of Mary as both mother and virgin. These roles are inherently incompatible, yet for generations Christianity has touted them as appropriate for a woman of faith. The church has often portrayed Mary as perfectly obedient and utterly responsive in offering herself to the (metaphorically) male Father. At times, sweet and innocent Mary has been figured as the "second Eve," who rights what the vilified Eve once wrought upon humanity. At other times, we have analyzed and assessed the details of the incarnation, trying to arrive at a plausible explanation. Some scholars have argued that Jesus' conception was anything but supernatural. Jane Schaberg, for example, has hypothesized that Mary was raped by a Roman soldier, but the Holy Spirit intervened to turn this child into God's son.[1] Others, such as Jürgen Moltmann, have emphasized the work of the Holy Spirit in the incarnation and minimized the role of Mary.[2] We have shaped, proclaimed, and debated these and other images of Mary, many of which stem not from the scriptural witnesses, but from later interpretations. In fact, we have scant information about the historical Mary and are unable to verify anything about her parents, her status in life, or even the portraits that come to us via the hands of the gospel writers. Despite all of this confusion, what the gospels suggest to us about Mary is crucial: she is among the earliest Godbearers, following the pattern revealed in Jesus.

According to tradition, one of the titles given to Mary is *Theotokos*, mother of God. *Theotokos* is intended to reflect the divinity of her child and the utter uniqueness of her motherhood. Yet Orthodox theologian Kallistos Ware has argued that the term *Theotokos* is more accurately translated as "Godbearer" than as "Mother of God."[3] It is this image of Mary as Godbearer, not only in the sense of being the physical bearer of God in Jesus, but also in reflecting the Christ character as it takes shape in the world, which we wish to explore more carefully in these pages.

Christians make the claim, of course, that Mary is the only human being to have literally borne God within. In the words of Robert Jenson, she makes a "space for God," and "her womb is the container of the uncontainable."[4] We tend to view her openness to God somewhat matter-of-factly, assuming that God must have preselected her due to her docile, passive, subservient nature. But, Mary had a choice to make; she had to respond to God's invitation to relationship out of her free will. When we turn to the text of Luke 1:26–38, we can detect in Mary an orientation or openness to the radical relationship offered by God, as well as a decision to enter into the fullness of Godbearing in the world.

In the story of Jesus' birth, Luke depicts Mary's encounter with the angel Gabriel. She is a young woman, a teenager at best, engaged to a man by the name of Joseph who would have needed only to negotiate the arrangements with her father in order to gain her hand. She possessed limited rights and voice in her society and quite possibly would have been predisposed to accept the societal roles and mores assigned to her. It is likely that her father had come to her one day and announced that she was to be married to this man Joseph at some future date, perhaps when she was a year or two older. The financial arrangements had already been negotiated; perhaps Joseph had paid the dowry. We do not know if Mary was pleased with the choice of Joseph or not; it was a matter over which she had little, if any, control. Of course, not all Jewish women in the first century conformed to the "idealized" norms established by the surviving ancient texts, and some women no doubt exercised considerable freedom beyond what was normally prescribed. This means we cannot comment with certainty on Mary's relationship to her family and her betrothed, though in general it is safe to say that throughout the ancient world—and much of the world today—women were assigned a subordinate role and place in life.

But when the angel disrupts Mary's ordinary life, the norms established by her society begin to reweave. The first thing we should note about this story is its radically relational character. Mary, the young woman with limited rights and voice, finds herself in the presence of God's messenger and is given the gift of agency. Here the text reveals a person of quiet strength, who does not approach this encounter meekly and is not stunned into silence. To the contrary, she finds her voice and questions the angel, both inwardly and outwardly, and dialogue ensues. God opens a space where Mary can act, speak, and decide—where she is not simply someone's property but is a person with agency. In this dialogical process, Mary arrives at her own conclusion and chooses to enter into radical relationship with God. God has given humanity the gift of free will, the gift to choose God's way or to go our own way, and Mary chooses to accept the invitation to be in radical relationship, just as each of us must choose to respond to grace. Is it possible that God had attempted to come into the world in the flesh before, in relationship with someone else who chose not to be a Godbearer? All we know is that this young woman, Mary, opened herself to God's overture: "Here am I," she announces, "the servant of the Lord; let it be with me according to your word" (Luke 1:38). With that, the angel is gone.

The text would almost have us think that this is a great and glorious decision for the young woman in which the sun bursts forth and alleluia choruses emanate from the heavens. But the choice is a decidedly risky one. There can be little doubt that she understood the consequences of being found pregnant when not yet married; after all, Joseph would know the child was not his. Her life would be ruined: her family shamed, her marriageability destroyed, her future marked by this living indiscretion. Did she tell her family and Joseph, or did they eventually see the evidence that she was pregnant? Did they become enraged and send her to stay with her relative, Elizabeth, for three months until they could decide what to do about the situation? The text does not provide the details, but Matthew tells us that Joseph had decided "to dismiss her quietly" (Matt. 1:19). After an angel appeared to Joseph in a dream, he changed his mind and remained in relationship with her. Although Joseph's response was less risky than Mary's, it was nonetheless uncommon according to societal standards. Both Mary and Joseph were sailing upon uncharted waters, opening their lives to God's grace, in spite of what people might think about them or what institutional structures expected. They had begun the process of reorientation toward radical relationship with God, self, others, and the whole of creation, though they did not know where this journey would lead them.

Surely this process disoriented Mary's expectations. In Luke the angel greets her with words of radical relationship: "The Lord is with you" (1:28). From her experience, she would have known that, according to the laws of Israel, only a male priest could enter into the holy of the holies and be in the presence of God. But incredibly, the angel tells her: God is with *you* in this place and time. Even more remarkable is the fact that the angel approaches a young woman to be the first Godbearer. This is not to suggest that somehow a man could have borne the infant in some odd twist of nature. But when a woman becomes the central figure in the story, given that it is a male-dominated society, we realize that God does not play according to the rules of society. In radical relationship with God, the powerless are empowered to give and receive the fullness of life. In fact, it is not long after Jesus' birth that Joseph, who by all societal norms should be the primary figure in this family and story, disappears completely from the narrative, while Mary remains present until the very end. Mary has chosen the way of the Godbearer, and the text testifies to the fact that anyone can become a participant in the life-centered discourse of God, if she is open to the possibility, chooses to respond, and is willing to be changed in the process.

Only as illuminated by this potential for entering into such radical relationship with God can we really grasp the meaning of the Magnificat or Mary's Song of Praise. She rejoices that God "has looked with favor on the lowliness of his servant" (Luke 1:47). But what kind of "favor" is this? When we, today, often associate the favor of God with material blessings and success, Mary's praise is utterly disorienting. The favor granted her is a pregnancy out of wedlock, the potential diminishment of her future, the shame of having to face the societal standards which label her "other" and "unrighteous." There is much about God's request that is anything but favorable according to the perspective of the world. Yet, what great favor for this one with limited status to be offered relationship and intimacy with God. Mary will contain the uncontainable within her body; she will make room for God even when the world refuses to do so. She will stay by Jesus' side, even when everyone else abandons him.

In Mary, then, we see something of the prototypical Godbearer among those who are born into the brokenness of human society. Her orientation toward Godbearing certainly is distinct from that of any other human being past, present, or future. Yet, in Mary's openness to radical relationship, she becomes a vital and enduring participant in the work of God in Christ in the Holy Spirit in the world. In Mary we see the renewed image of God blossoming within her. Even though Mary is asked to take on a rather traditional role—that of mother—her story casts motherhood in a new light. It turns the notion of the pure and innocent virgin upside down, for this chaste child becomes the bearer of the gift of salvation coming into the world. Mary opens a space within herself for the reconciliation of humanity and God to take shape, and she opens the way for God to renew and reorient a broken world. In the process, Mary, herself, is reoriented to the giving and receiving of life.

Mary also bears faithful witness to God in her words and actions, revealing the strength of body and spirit found in and through relationship with God. We hear her speaking prophetically in the Magnificat, testifying to the message and the ministry that will be present in Jesus her son: bringing mercy to those who fear (in the sense of having "awe" before) God, bringing down the powerful of the world and lifting up the lowly, filling the hungry with good things while sending the rich away empty, and fulfilling God's promises. Perhaps the widespread popular devotion to Mary can be credited, at least in part, to the faithful witness she continues to bear to people throughout the world. One of the most striking examples of Marian devotion is found in Mexico, where *Nuestra Señora de Guadalupe*, Our Lady of Guadalupe, serves as a symbol of strength and hope for the poor and oppressed, echoing the testimony that God lifts the lowly and fills the hungry. Mary's witness tells us that faithfulness to God does not mean our lives will become perfect, painless, or predictable. But it demonstrates the powerful testimony our words and lives can offer when we receive and share the life of God.

Finally, when we read the scriptures and acknowledge the importance of Mary's witness to countless Christians, we see that she also bears the suffering of others. In the gospels, Mary stands near the cross, refusing to abandon her beloved son. Historically, Mary has helped others to bear their suffering in the world, not only in the image of *Guadalupe,* but also, for example, among Coptic Orthodox women in Egypt who view Mary as "a source of consolation to mothers who identify with her troubles as a refugee who fled to Egypt to save the life of her baby and as a mother who saw her son unjustly murdered."[5] Similarly, for the many loved ones of *los desaparecidos* ("the disappeared") throughout Latin America, Mary's witness enables them to bear their suffering as they search for answers, refusing to let their loved ones be abandoned and forgotten.

In many ways Mary epitomizes the attitude of the Godbearer who cradles the brokenness of others in her arms and shares in their suffering at the hands of a death-dealing world: in the artistic expressions of the *Pieta,* Mary bears in her lap the broken body of her crucified son, the One who is all of us, the One who is fully human. Perhaps from the annunciation and the birth of Jesus, who was the expected Messiah, Mary had awaited the moment of his emergence as the great warrior-king, the new David. To have remained present to her son throughout his painful rejection by the people of Israel and his excruciating death on the cross, humiliated and abandoned by almost all of his followers, was an act of radical relationship. This image of Mary bearing the lifeless body of her beloved son symbolizes the bearing of suffering to which each of us is called. We cannot bring the injustice and pain of the world to an end, but we can stand with and beside those who suffer, helping them to bear their difficulties and pointing toward the radical relationship that has promised to make all things new.

MARY MAGDALENE, APOSTLE TO THE APOSTLES, GODBEARER

Mary Magdalene provides us with a second striking biblical image of Godbearing. In some ways, Mary Magdalene has been viewed as the antithesis of Jesus' mother Mary. In the West, she has been depicted for generations as a fallen and redeemed woman: a prostitute, an adulteress, a sinner whose tears wash Jesus' feet. Scholars today widely agree that the New Testament does not support these characterizations, which have often drawn upon texts referring to unnamed women and assigned them to Mary of Magdala. In the Eastern tradition of the church, she has been called the apostle to the apostles or the one who shares the good news of the resurrection. This second image conveys what we might consider another early model of Godbearing, and one that is consistent with the scriptural witnesses.

What does the New Testament tell us about Mary Magdalene and how do the texts describe her in ways that are consistent with the pattern of Godbearing? The Gospel of Luke tells us that Jesus had cured Mary, called Magdalene, of seven demons, but nothing more is said about the nature of her illness (8:2). Indeed, contrary to the tradition that has painted her as the penitent prostitute, "[b]eing possessed by 'seven demons' that were exorcised by Jesus, she was arguably more victim than sinner."[6] More importantly, Mary was among the women who, along with the twelve disciples, accompanied Jesus as he traveled "through cities and villages, proclaiming the good news of the kingdom of God" (Luke 8:1). Magdalene, as well as these other women who followed Jesus, such as the wife of Herod's steward and Susanna, "provided for them out of their resources" (8:3). This note suggests that Mary may have been a woman of some means who contributed financially to the ministry of Jesus. In any case, there can be little doubt that she was a disciple who participated in Jesus' ministry, though "there is no narrative of her call, nor any narrative in which she plays an active role or speaks or is spoken to in the ministry."[7]

When we turn to Luke's resurrection narrative, we watch as Mary Magdalene, along with Joanna and Mary, the mother of James, arrive at Jesus' tomb on the first day of the week only to find the tomb empty. The women are spoken to by "two men in dazzling white clothes" (Luke 24:4), who proclaim to them, "Remember how he told you, while he was still in Galilee, that the Son of Man must be handed over to sinners, and be crucified, and on the third day rise again" (Luke 24:7). Significantly, in Luke 9, Jesus foretells his death and resurrection while alone "with only the disciples" (v. 18). This announcement, "Remember how he told *you,*" seems to reinforce that the women were among Jesus' most intimate followers. Luke 2:2 explicitly names Mary, called Magdalene, as among the women traveling with him as he proclaims the good news in cities and villages. Perhaps she was among the seventy sent out by Jesus. In any case, it is clear that Jesus told only his closest followers of his impending death and resurrection, and in all likelihood, Mary Magdalene had heard these word while following him.

The other gospels also place Mary Magdalene at the tomb, as the first witness to the resurrection. In Matthew she arrives with "the other Mary" (Matt. 28:1) and after being greeted by the angel, they "go quickly and tell his disciples" as the angel commands (v. 7). In Mark, it is Mary Magdalene, Mary the mother of James, and Salome who go to the tomb and find Jesus is not there (Mark 16). But they "went out and fled from the tomb, for terror and amazement had seized them; and they said nothing to anyone for they were afraid" (v. 8). Although some ancient authorities suggest that the original gospel ended after verse 8, in other ancient manuscript traditions and the canonical version, we find that the risen Jesus first appears to Mary of Magdala, who then goes and announces the news to the grieving disciples (Mark 16:9–11). In the Gospel of John, Jesus first appears to Mary Magdalene, who initially mistakes him for the gardener (John 20:11–18). She is, in fact, the first person to whom the risen Christ speaks, and he concludes by telling her to go to his "brothers" (v. 17). Although in the longer ending of Mark and in Luke, Mary Magdalene's testimony is initially discounted until confirmed by male disciples, the Gospel of John suggests that her announcement was taken to heart. After all, she "went and announced to the disciples, 'I have seen the Lord'; and she told them that he had said these things to her" (John 20:18). Unlike Mark and Luke, John does not make the claim that her testimony was not believed. Perhaps Mark and Luke did not intend to convey that a *woman's* word was not believable, but rather, that anyone who might have first announced the risen Christ would have lacked credibility. After all, they had seen Jesus die, and they had not seen him rise again. Moreover, in the end, the scriptures prove that Mary Magdalene was bearing faithful witness to God and that her proclamation was valid. It was Jesus himself who appointed her as apostle to the apostles. Her call to proclaim the resurrection of Jesus was given to her by God, despite societal norms and expectations.

What is striking about the scriptural witnesses is that Mary Magdalene is the only person named in all four accounts as the first to see the tomb empty and learn of Jesus' resurrection. Jesus' mother, Mary, first bore Jesus to the world, bringing him to life in the flesh. Now, at the end of the gospels, Mary Magdalene bears Jesus to the world, announcing his restored life and the renewed possibility of relationship. One is the principal Godbearer at the incarnation; the other the principal Godbearer at the resurrection. In the witness of Magdalene, we find the message of radical relationship with God that overcomes the brokenness of the world and restores and upholds the fullness of life. The scriptural witnesses concerning Mary Magdalene suggest to us that her life embodied Jesus' call to be a Godbearer in the world.

In light of the above contention that Magdalene, like Jesus' mother, bears Jesus to the world, we can grasp how she bears God within. Indeed, we might suggest that the renewed image of God in Mary of Magdala begins when Jesus heals her of the seven demons. To draw out this point, before being healed by Jesus, Mary Magdalene "was considered a victim of a disease not easily understandable, which took her over physically and psychically, completely (shown by the use of the number seven) . . ."[8] Mary was broken, physically, mentally, and in all likelihood, spiritually. Perhaps she was filled with self-loathing. Quite possibly she was shunned by society. Her healing by Jesus of Nazareth reoriented her existence, not only moving her from brokenness to greater wholeness, but also transforming her daily existence. As Carla Ricci notes, "beyond the unknowable specific details of her cure, Mary Magdalene, a woman 'dispossessed of herself,' came back from Jesus as a woman restored to herself, to the depths of her own being. And perhaps rather than one central moment, there was a process, a developing relationship of discovery and growth."[9] In Mary Magdalene we experience the restoration of relationship as she moves from isolation to life in and with God, herself, others, and perhaps, the whole of creation. As this renewed reality grasps Mary Magdalene, she reorients her life and begins to follow Jesus and to participate in his ministry. In this dramatic reorientation to giving and receiving life, Mary Magdalene bears the renewed image of God within. She is transformed and continues to be transformed by this radical relationship.

While Mary increasingly bore the image of God within, there can be little doubt that she participated in bearing faithful witness to God. Indeed, this is the role most clearly assigned to Mary Magdalene by the scriptures and later interpreters. As the "apostle to the apostles," as the first witness to the resurrection, Mary immediately testifies to what she has seen and heard. She runs to the disciples to share the good news. Whether or not she is believed initially, whether or not others embrace the message she brings, Mary Magdalene does not refrain from speaking the word of God. She has been called and commanded by God to bear witness, and she responds. It is particularly significant that the "voice" and the testimony of Mary Magdalene continue to be heard, since the gospels were written and canonized under the auspices of a male-dominated society. Against all odds, Mary Magdalene continues to bear faithful witness to the giving and receiving of life in and through Jesus Christ. We would not be exaggerating to speak of Mary Magdalene as one of Christianity's earliest and longest serving preachers of the good news. In any case, as the apostle to the apostles, she saw the empty tomb and the risen Christ and shared the good news with the other disciples. Century after century, on Christianity's holiest Sunday, Mary Magdalene rises from the gospels as the first witness to life overcoming death.

Despite attempts by the later church to cast Mary Magdalene into the role of sinner and dismiss the significance of her relationship to Jesus, her testimony survives. This woman was not timid about speaking publicly of her life in God in Christ in the Holy Spirit nor was she reluctant to reorient her life to follow Jesus. Instead, against all odds and various societal prohibitions, Mary Magdalene proclaimed Christ's way and lived out the calling to radical discipleship, and she continues to bear faithful witness to us today.

Finally, Mary Magdalene also bears with God the suffering of others. She stands at a distance watching Jesus' agonizing death on Golgotha. Unable to bring him down from the cross, she refuses to leave Jesus—and perhaps the other women disciples and his mother,

Mary—to suffer alone. Perhaps she held Jesus' mother as she sobbed under the unbearable weight of the cross. Perhaps Mary Magdalene remained close enough that Jesus could see her from a distance, comforted by the knowledge that not all the disciples had abandoned and denied him in his most difficult moment. At the same time, on another level, Mary Magdalene shares in the suffering of countless people throughout the ages who have been marginalized, silenced, and unjustly demonized. Relegated to the margins throughout much of Christian history, depicted not so much as a faithful follower of Jesus, but as a harlot, Mary of Magdala shares in the reality of many others past and present who have been unfairly condemned by the powerful in society. Mary Magdalene is the man on death row who is released after new DNA evidence vindicates his innocence. Mary Magdalene is the Guatemalan immigrant crossing the border under cover of darkness, joining hundreds of thousands to protest inhumane legislation, refusing to let death-dealing conditions starve her family of the dream of life and dignity. Mary Magdalene is the single mother who works three minimum-wage jobs to provide the basics for her children while her ex-husband refuses to pay court-ordered child support. Mary Magdalene's healing and recovery, in recent years, from demonization by the tradition also provides hope for those who experience marginalization and social barriers and constructions of identity that limit their ability to respond fully to God's call. Mary Magdalene proclaims the power of life over death, which is found in faithfully following the crucified and risen Christ. Participating in the life-giving and receiving reality of God, Mary Magdalene rises from the ashes as one of the earliest examples of Godbearing in the Christian tradition.

PAUL, APOSTLE TO THE GENTILES, GODBEARER

Finally, in our brief consideration of Godbearing in the scriptures, we cannot neglect Saul of Tarsus, who became Paul, the apostle to the Gentiles and the first Christian theologian. It is quite possible that the tradition has also treated Paul unfairly, misrepresenting his words and actions in order to conform to later standards of the church and society. For example, in recent decades, scholars have questioned whether Paul's instructions about women in 1 Corinthians

14:33b–36 are actually a later insertion into his letter, especially given the prominence of women, such as Phoebe, in his ministry. Although we will have more to say in the following chapter about the notion of "conversion," Saul's reorientation toward the radical relationality of God provides another important witness to and model of the practice of Godbearing.

Our portrait of Paul emerges not in the Gospels, but in the Acts of the Apostles and by Paul's own hand in his correspondence to the early communities of faith. Here, the Book of Acts provides us with the "outsider's" view of Paul's life and ministry as a Godbearer, which complements his own words. We know that he was a devout Jew, a Pharisee, a prominent member of the community, and a persecutor of Jesus' followers in Jerusalem, that he encountered the risen Christ along the road to Damascus, and—however we may assess it—that he became one of the most important figures in the spread of the Christian faith. Yet, at the same time, when we investigate Paul in terms of his attitude toward bearing God within, bearing faithful witness to God, and bearing the suffering of others, he appears in a new light. Paul travels the way of Godbearing.

In considering Paul's orientation toward bearing the renewed image of God within, we turn first to his Damascus road experience. Traditionally, we have viewed this event as Paul's "conversion" experience, though it would be more appropriate to speak of his reorientation toward the giving and receiving of life in its fullness. Upon closer examination, we become aware that Paul's reorientation is a lifelong process of growing into the Christ character. There is evidence that Saul engaged in violent acts, breathed "threats and murder against the disciples of the Lord" (Acts 9:1), "was ravaging the church by entering house after house; dragging off both men and women, he committed them to prison" (Acts 8:3). Here we are not suggesting any causal relationship between Saul's religious commitments and his violence against followers of Jesus. After all, Jesus himself was a Jew. Rather, we are pointing toward something deep within him that clings to the world's brokenness. Saul of Tarsus engaged in violent acts that perpetuated and deepened the world's brokenness, despite his commitment to God's law and way—an orientation we can detect in some persons who claim to follow Christ in our own time. Paul was a man who believed in God and had dedicated his life to his religious community, but Paul had not taken to heart the scriptural commandments that suggest the love of God and caring for others are central to God's way. His whole being was not yet oriented toward the giving and receiving of life.

Saul's encounter with and response to the risen Christ along the road to Damascus reoriented his life in crucial ways and led him to enter into the practice of Godbearing in the world. First, Paul begins to reflect the renewed image of God, though the change was a gradual process in which, over time, Paul was formed into the Christ character and began to bear more fully the image of God within. Acts 13:9 provides the first reference to Saul as Paul, and the story that follows depicts a man who continues to display a certain amount of harshness.[10] While in Cyprus with Barnabas, Paul encounters the magician and false prophet Bar-Jesus who tries to block them from sharing the good news with the proconsul Sergius Paulus. Paul invokes the wrath of God against Bar-Jesus and enshrouds him in mist and darkness so that he might be blind for a while (13:10–11). Such a response is hardly consistent with the teaching and ministry of Jesus of Nazareth who is the Christ, though it echoes Paul's own blindness along the road. Here the axiom about the blind leading the blind seems appropriate.

In Acts 19, we find Paul in Ephesus for two years, speaking boldly and arguing persuasively about the kingdom of God (v. 8). "When some stubbornly refused to believe and spoke evil of the Way before the congregation, [Paul] left them, taking the disciples with him" (v. 9). In this case, it seems that rather than lashing out at his detractors, Paul withdraws from the situation. Then, in Acts 20, while Paul is in Troas, a young man named Eutychus, is sitting in a window and falls asleep while Paul is talking (v. 9). He tumbles three stories to the ground and appears dead. Paul goes down, picks up the young man in his arms, and announces, "Do not be alarmed, for his life is in him." Here Paul demonstrates the giving and receiving of life so characteristic of Jesus. Indeed, after holding the man, Paul goes back upstairs and breaks bread with those in the meeting room (v. 11). They enter into communion with one another, and we are told that the young man lived.

Soon the tables begin to turn and Paul finds himself among the persecuted, with violence being waged against him. Rather than fighting back, he asks to address the people (Acts 21). He speaks to them about his blinding encounter with the risen Christ and how he then met the man, Ananias, who restored his sight while telling him, "you will be his witness to all the world of what you have seen and heard" (Acts 22:15). Forced to appear before the governor, Felix, at Caesarea, Paul "cheerfully" offers his defense (24:10) before being placed in custody. He remains imprisoned for more than two years, and when he is finally allowed to plead his case before King Agrippa, Paul testifies to his encounter with the risen Christ on the road to Damascus and his preaching throughout Judea and to the Gentiles "that they should repent and turn to God and do deeds consistent with repentance" (Acts 26:20).

Following his release, while sailing for Rome, the ship encounters a raging storm. Paul remains calm through the turbulent days and nights, and on the fourteenth day, just before daybreak, he urges the sailors to take some food: "it will help you survive; for none of you will lose a hair from your heads" (Acts 27:34). Then Paul takes bread, gives thanks to God, breaks the bread, and begins to eat, which encourages the others to do likewise. In this act of communion, Paul again enters fully into the giving and receiving of life. The last we see of Paul, he is on the island of Malta and cures the father of Publius "by praying and putting his hands on him" (Acts 28:8). Thus, as we reach the end of the Book of Acts, Paul has been reoriented toward the giving and receiving of life. His harshness in lashing out against the magician shortly after his encounter with the risen Christ stands in stark contrast to the acts of communion and healing that we see much later in his discipleship. In the words of Frederick Buechner, "Paul sets out a hatchet man . . . and comes back a fool for Christ."[11] Paul enters into a gradual process of being formed in the Christ character and expressing this orientation outwardly. We might say that Paul's radical relationship with God enables the renewed image of God to be borne and to grow within him.

Because our lives in Christ unfold as a journey, we are often startled to see our own gradual Paul-like transformation over the years. At times this recognition takes the form of dramatic, "see-how-sinful-I-used-to-be" testimonials, but a simple before-and-after pattern such as this is often misleading. It is not as if we believe in Christ and suddenly find ourselves expressing perfect relationship with God, self, others, and creation. Throughout our lives, if we remain open to God, we will find ourselves renewed and reoriented into a fuller expression of the Christ character. Like a child at birth, year by year we mature and learn more about who we are in relationship to God. For example, over time we might become convinced that we no longer need the four-bedroom, three-bath home with the two-car garage that consumes precious energy resources. We decide to downsize to a more modest space. Perhaps we commit ourselves to something as simple as buying fair trade coffee at a higher price or volunteering at the local animal shelter. Or maybe we accept leadership positions in our church and give up some of our free time or, conversely, we let go of some of our leadership positions and spend more time attending to our spiritual disciplines and other relationships. Across the landscape of our lives, we find ourselves expressing in greater measure and more simple, ordinary ways our orientation to God in Christ in the Holy Spirit. Paul's example gives us evidence of what it means to bear God within ourselves.

The scriptures also provide considerable evidence of Paul's orientation toward bearing faithful witness to God. His public proclamation of the fullness of life in Jesus Christ is documented in both the Acts of the Apostles and Paul's own letters. Some passages penned by Paul are among the greatest found in literature: Romans 8:35–39, 1 Corinthians 13, and Philippians 2:1–11, to name a few. Even more noteworthy is the life Paul led and the witness it continues to bear to his relationship with God. Saul of Tarsus was, in all likelihood, a man of some means who lived a life of relative privilege among the more influential members of his Jewish community and as a Roman citizen. In reorienting his life toward God in Christ in the Holy Spirit, he accepted a much different role. Paul became subject to imprisonment, torture, persecution, isolation, the hardships of constant travel, and the homelessness of an itinerant missionary. Although he remained human and subject to the brokenness of existence—for example, becoming "obsessed with the threat to his own apostolate by Jewish 'super-apostles'"—the depths of his reorientation are striking, even two thousand years later.[12] Paul understood that life in God does not lead to increasing riches or power; he knew that life in God would not make him superior to others. He accepted that life in Christ meant renouncing the accumulation of material possessions, entering into the messiness of community in the *ekklesia* or assembly of those called out of society and into the body of Christ, and opposing the imperial designs of "the rulers of this age." Paul grasped that radical relationship with God, self, others, and creation is embedded in the giving and receiving of life for the mutual well-being of the whole. In the many expressions of his life, Paul demonstrated a commitment to God's way and bore faithful witness to the life-centered discourse of Christ.

Finally, Paul's actions demonstrate how thoroughly he entered into bearing with God the suffering of others. We know that Paul continually worked to collect funds for the "poor among the saints in Jerusalem" (Rom. 15:26) and viewed this redistribution of resources as a gift of and to the glory of God (2 Cor. 9). Here Paul insists that sharing resources, rather than accumulating and hoarding them, is central to the fullness of life. In his tireless efforts to provide for the needs of the poor, he entered into their suffering and sought to ameliorate it as much as possible. Paul opposed the imperial powers of Rome and worked to establish communities that expressed the radical relationality of God. Horsley argues:

> Paul insisted . . . that his *ekklesiai* should be exclusive communities, open to recruiting from, but otherwise not participating in, wider imperial society, whether in civil courts or in temple banquets (1 Cor. 5:9–13; 6:1–11; and 10:14–22, respectively). Of course, he expected the imminent end of "this evil age," of "this world which is passing away." Meanwhile, evidently anticipating a continuation of some sort of societal form of "the kingdom of God," he was busy forming "assemblies" in the cities of the eastern empire as communities alternative to the existing society. . . . However vague he was about social forms in "the kingdom of God" which was presumably coming at the "day of the Lord" and

> (the completion of) the resurrection, in his mission Paul was building an international alternative society (the "assembly") based on local egalitarian communities ("assemblies").[13]

We should not forget, as noted in previous chapters, that Paul proclaimed a new identity in Christ, an identity in which relationships that diminish the flourishing of life are overturned. In the already-but-not-yet of the reign of God on earth, Paul grasped the importance of mutuality and solidarity within the body of Christ, seeking the mutual upbuilding of all who followed this Way. Indeed, Paul opened himself to suffering that he could have avoided had he remained in his more privileged role in society. But Christian faith is not a call to the comfortable life. Quite the contrary, it is an unsettling existence in which our ongoing reorientation toward radical relationship creates discomfort vis-à-vis cultural standards and priorities. We are no longer comfortable acting in the old ways—not simply in a moral sense, but more importantly, in a socially conscious, justice-seeking, life-giving and -receiving sense. We are no longer comfortable living our lives in God for one or perhaps two hours each week, and pursuing the "American dream" the other 167 hours, turning our backs on the genocide that cries out from Africa, "Why have you abandoned me?" We are no longer content to follow Christ on Sunday and the pursuit of economic "happiness" the other six days, while children across the United States go to bed hungry. Paul urges us with both his words and actions to "bear one another's burdens" (Gal. 6:2) and to accept that receiving the fullness of life also means giving of ourselves that others might live. In his attitude toward bearing God within, bearing faithful witness, and bearing the suffering of others, Paul demonstrates his gradual reorientation toward radical relationship with God, self, others, and creation.

Our brief consideration of Godbearing in the scriptures does not begin to do justice to the extent of the witnesses to the giving and receiving of life for those who follow God in Christ in the Holy Spirit. Yet it provides us with a basis for grasping the fullness of life reoriented toward radical relationship. We have seen that as our lives are reoriented and the Christ character takes shape within us, we begin to bear God's image within ourselves and to bear faithful witness to others, as well as their sufferings in the world. The pattern of Godbearing that we find in the scriptures has found expression in history as well, and when we consider the lives of historical persons, we come even closer to grasping how we, too, can become Godbearers in the world. Undoubtedly, countless persons throughout history have entered into the practice of Godbearing, but many of those led quiet, unheralded lives of radical relationship and were known only to those whose lives they touched. Yet, a few figures continue to express the reality of Godbearing across time and space. Two such figures are Bartolomé de Las Casas and Rosa Parks. Las Casas and Parks help to redirect our vision toward both the obvious and the more subtle expressions of God's way in the world and show us how we, too, might become Godbearers who express the heights and depths of the gospel in our world.

BARTOLOMÉ DE LAS CASAS, GODBEARER

In prophetic fashion, an early-sixteenth century priest battles against the powerful Spanish military and political presence in Latin America, as it perpetrates violence against and imposes servitude upon the indigenous people. He rails against the system of slavery that massacres the innocent and lines the coffers of people halfway around the globe: "Tell me, by what right or justice do you keep these Indians in such a cruel and horrible servitude? On what authority have you waged a detestable war against these people?"[14] He sacrifices his own status, income, position, and comfort to denounce the death-dealing pursuit of wealth and power under the auspices of Christian mission and evangelization. The story of Bartolomé de Las Casas is one of service and openness to God, self, others, and creation that led toward ongoing reorientation to radical relationship and away from the societal standards of his day. Today, Las Casas symbolizes the struggle for liberation from destructive, death-dealing colonial powers.

Born in Spain in 1484, Las Casas witnessed firsthand the celebrations following Christopher Columbus's initial journey to the Americas.[15] Although he was born of humble means, Las Casas' family was relatively privileged by the time he entered college, his father having joined the ranks of the wealthy as a result of traveling to the

New World on Columbus's second voyage. Before completing his studies in canon law and entering the priesthood, Las Casas made his first journey to Santa Domingo in 1502 and spent five years traveling with military expeditions, witnessing the massacre of indigenous peoples. Deeply disturbed by this violence, he began to question the practice. He deplored the conditions under which the Native Americans were forced to live, especially their enslavement by the Spaniards in the *encomienda* system of forced labor. Las Casas recognized that foremost in the hearts and minds of the Spaniards who traveled to Hispaniola was this desire to acquire gold on the backs of the native miners. Though he remained reluctant to speak or act publicly at this point, something in Las Casas began to turn toward life in radical relationship over death-dealing practices. Reorientation had begun to take place deep within him.

After returning to Spain in 1506, Las Casas completed his studies in canon law and was ordained a priest. He then set sail once again for the New World intending to serve as the official catechist to the natives. In spite of his earlier voyage and the discomfort he had experienced, he continued to participate in the brutal enslavement of others and the comfortable life it afforded him. "Like many other Spaniards in the West Indies, including clerics, he lived off the toil of the Indians of his *encomienda*—the system by which Spanish colonists were given tracts of land and the rights to the forced labor of the native people in return for a promise to instruct them in the faith."[16] We can almost hear Las Casas rationalizing, "I'm only one man, under the authority of others. What can I do? I can't change the world. Besides, I'm saving their souls." Although in the service of God, Las Casas—not unlike the apostle Paul—at least implicitly supported death-dealing social and cultural standards that perpetuated the way of brokenness in the world.

Gradually the direction of Las Casas' life shifted. His apparent openness to God began to turn him away from those death-dealing social and cultural practices and toward life-centered relationship with God, self, others, and creation. For years, Las Casas had witnessed the atrocities against the native peoples and even heard Dominican friars condemn the *encomienda* system, but he remained unmoved until 1514 when he experienced "a profound conversion of conscience."[17] The lovelessness of the Spaniards' practices began to take its toll on Las Casas' spirit and psyche, despite the ways in which he benefited personally from the colonial system. Thus, on Pentecost Sunday, he "renounced his ownership of Indians and the inter-island provisions business. He then started to preach his own provocative sermons against the wrongs of the conquest, particularly the *encomienda* system."[18] Not only did he reorient his life and his way of relating to the indigenous peoples, but he began to advocate on their behalf, as he now "saw that everything the Spaniards had done in the Indies from the beginning—all the brutal exploitation and decimation of innocent Indians, with no heed for their welfare or their conversion—was not only completely wrong, but also mortal sin."[19]

From that time forward, Las Casas engaged in a bitter struggle against the colonial systems and people who destroyed the natives' lives and well-being for the sake of personal and societal gain. He argued forcefully for the rights of the indigenous population in the New World, claiming that all people are made in the image of God and that the human race is one family. Arguments such as these have led legal scholar Paolo Carozza to suggest that Las Casas "embodied" or symbolized the birth of the modern idea of human rights.[20] "Las Casas succeeded in articulating and advocating a set of ideas that in many senses represents the first clear announcement of the modern language of human rights."[21] We might go so far as to identify Las Casas as a forerunner of the liberation theologians who arose in the 1960s, since his theological and practical struggle for justice was not unlike what arose on the same landscape some four centuries later.

Throughout his writings, Las Casas criticizes the abuse of the natives at the hands of "good" Christians intent on converting the "heathens." He does not hesitate to identify the link between Christian mission and economic gain. For example, in his "Brief Account of the Devastation of the Indies" (1542), Las Casas lambastes the Spaniards: "Their reason for killing and destroying such an infinite number of souls is that the Christians have an ultimate aim, which is to acquire gold, and to swell themselves with riches in a very brief time and thus rise to a high estate disproportionate to their merits. It should be kept in mind that their insatiable greed and ambition, the greatest ever seen in the world, is the cause of their villainies."[22] In his unfinished *History of the Indies,* Las Casas hoped to "call the attention of the readers to the terrifying disparity between the missionary purpose of the encounter between Christian Europeans and Native Americans and the brutal exploitation of the second by the first."[23] He also sought to "proclaim the humanity of the indigenous peoples, their rationality, their personal and collective freedom," and "to record a dissenting testimony with the hope that his *History* will one day be read, by future generations or even maybe at the eschatological moment of reckoning."[24]

Today, Latin Americans, in particular, draw upon Las Casas' advocacy to continue the work of human rights in the postcolonial era. Yet, the church in the United States would do well to heed the witness of Las Casas in its search for renewal. He points us toward the flourishing of life as one human community in radical relationship to God. His testimony demonstrates the possibility of "conversion" from the temptations of society with its political and economic ambitions to the way of God in Christ in the Holy Spirit. If we consider Las Casas from the perspective of Godbearing, we can see that he bore within himself the renewed image of God and came to see its presence in all human beings, no matter their race, culture, language, or worldview. In recognizing the image of God in the Native Americans, Las Casas reminds us that all people are beloved children of God. The image of God in us embraces the image of God in the other or, to paraphrase a more common axiom, the life of Christ in us upholds the life of Christ in all.

At the same time, Las Casas' bears faithful witness to God. He unflinchingly exposed the injustice and violence of the colonial "Christian" powers for what they were: loveless pursuers of wealth and dominance at the expense of others and the creation, greedy robbers stealing territory that was not theirs to possess. Las Casas' life and words testify that it is not enough to claim to be a follower of Christ. It is not enough to travel to distant lands to convert others in the name of God, while justifying our own desires for power and wealth as God's will. Even four hundred years later, Las Casas' faithful witness continues to raise questions about the occupation of lands, the stripping of precious resources, and the lack of care for the human family under the neocolonial systems that exist in today's world.

Finally, in turning from a life of privilege supported by the system of forced labor, Las Casas entered into the suffering of others, sharing the burden that had been imposed upon them. There can be little doubt that Las Casas himself suffered for his reorientation toward the enslaved Americans. In fact, the more intense his advocacy became, the "more enmeshed in scandal and controversy. He had his *Confesionario*—the rules for confessors that he had composed—confiscated because it insisted that every penitent be required to free his Indian slaves and make full restitution of all the Spaniards' unjustly acquired wealth in the New World. This seemed to call into question the very legitimacy of Spain's claim to rule the Indies, and Las Casas was accused of treason."[25] Clearly, Las Casas suffered personal loss and difficulties as his life became more deeply directed toward the way of God in the world. Yet it was far more important to him to share the burden of suffering with the native peoples and to advocate for their release from captivity than it was to be personally comfortable and privileged at their expense. He could not turn away from their brokenness or how his own life contributed to it. He did not shrug his shoulders and capitulate to a system that was far more powerful than one small cleric could ever hope to be. Instead, by the grace of God, he acted in every possible way to transform death-dealing systems into life-centered ones. Las Casas retraces the image of the pieta, as he holds the broken bodies and lives of the American peoples, tenderly caring for them, unwilling to let injustice remain unchallenged. Today, Bartolomé de Las Casas, in his words and deeds, continues to serve the radical relationality of God in our own cultural and historical moment.

ROSA PARKS, GODBEARER

In October 2005, the flag-draped coffin of a seamstress and social activist lay in state under the rotunda of the Capitol building as mourners streamed past to pay their respects. Most of them had never met her in person; they knew her only as a symbol and an agent of transformative justice within a society whose laws and practices had once categorized African Americans as "inferior" and "second-class" citizens with "separate but equal" rights. It was a remarkable moment: for the first time in U.S. history, an African American woman who had grasped power in the midst of powerlessness and risen up in peaceful resistance was honored in the manner of presidents and other high officials. Yet, in 1955, she could not walk through the front door of most restaurants, could not attend the college of her choice, and could not even drink from the nearby water fountain unless it was marked with the word, "Colored." For persons born in the 1960s and later, it is almost impossible to comprehend the extent of the death-dealing, life-diminishing practices that were normative in the southern United States, the so-called "Bible belt," before civil rights legislation. Yet, this woman's openness to God and the life-giving and receiving way of Christ ultimately led her to engage in an act of civil disobedience that would help to inspire the nation to reorient its laws and practices in favor of inclusion, dignity, and life for all persons—though the process of reorientation is not yet finished even fifty years later. The flag-draped coffin resting quietly in the rotunda, under the watchful eye of a uniformed man protecting rather than arresting the woman, seemed to whisper, "Look how far we've come . . . and how far we have to go."

Rosa Parks was an ordinary woman who, as a young child, "learned from the Bible to trust in God and not be afraid."[26] There was nothing in her upbringing or circumstances that destined her to become an agent of change and a social activist, nothing she points to in her autobiography that steered her in this direction, except perhaps her lifelong engagement with the life of faith and the steady courage and strength of her family.[27] Parks claims that her grandfather never seemed to show fear, even when the Ku Klux Klan was in the neighborhood.[28] She writes that her mother, "used to always tell me that all of God's children were supposed to be free. She kept telling me this over and over again until I truly felt that one day we would be free, because God had meant for it to be this way."[29] Perhaps Parks would not have been actively involved in the civil rights movement had it not been "closely tied to the church in its fight against injustice."[30]

On December 1, 1955, the bus on which Parks was riding epitomized the lived reality of the racial divisions in the United States. Riding the bus was a constant reminder that all were equal in the eyes of God but not in the eyes of the state or even those of many "faithful" Christians. With the bus segregated according to skin color, Parks was seated in the first row of the "colored" section when the "white" section became full. Because the separation was intended to signal binary distinctions such as superior and inferior, the African Americans were expected to give up their seats to their "superiors," even though she was within her legal rights to sit in that row. The bus driver demanded that Parks and others give up their seats, so the "white" section could be expanded to accommodate more riders. The man sitting next to her complied, as did the women across the aisle, but Parks remained unmoved. She was tired, and her act of civil disobedience was the spark that ignited the nation, though the tinder had long been primed to erupt.

Although this story of Rosa Parks is familiar to most U.S. citizens, it is often told with a revisionist sensibility; that is, people often claim that on that landmark day in 1955, she did not move from her seat on the bus because she was physically tired. Indeed, Rosa Parks was tired, but it was the segregation and racism of the nation that made her tired:

> When I sat down on the bus the day I was arrested, I was thinking of going home. I had made up my mind quickly about what it was that I had to do, what I felt was right to do. I did not think of being physically tired or fearful. After so many years of oppression and being a victim of the mistreatment that my people had suffered, not giving up my seat—and whatever I had to face after not giving it up—was not important. . . . All I felt was tired. Tired of being pushed around. Tired of seeing the bad treatment and disrespect of children, women, and men just because of the color of their skin. Tired of the Jim Crow laws. Tired of being oppressed.[31]

Parks had been active in the NAACP and, in the summer of 1955, had attended a workshop in Tennessee on racial desegregation. Unbeknownst to many, she was not the first woman arrested for refusing to give up her seat on a bus, but her case proved to be the right test of the law at the right point in history. Because Parks embraced the fullness of life over death-dealing systems, the

Montgomery bus boycott was launched. Her sense of justice in the face of institutionalized racism, no matter the personal cost, gave others the courage to join in the struggle. In the end, the boycott did effect change in the public bus system, though Parks could not have known how her decision would unfold over time. Moreover, throughout her life she maintained that people gave her too much credit for launching the bus boycott.[32] Yet, by faith in God, it was Rosa Parks who remained seated that day, who rested on the good news and promise of God's radical relationship that overcomes the world's brokenness.

Unlike Las Casas, there was no distinct "conversion" experience that led Parks to remain seated on that bus. Nor did she experience a mystical vision, a miraculous healing, or angels announcing that God was with her, as did so many biblical Godbearers. Instead, in her story we can detect a gradual and continuous reorientation across her lifetime. Despite being born into a society that labeled her "inferior," forced her to live in conditions that obstructed the flourishing of her full humanity, and treated her as less than human, Parks remained open to God's grace. As a young child, her family introduced her to faith in God, and the black church testified and affirmed that she was a child of God no matter what society claimed. Over time, the Christ character took shape within her, and Parks's identity was formed, not by the world's standards, but by and through radical relationship with God, self, others, and creation. Over time and through faith in God, she became reoriented toward the giving and receiving of life. Over time, rather than in an instant, she became an agent of social transformation beyond what seemed humanly possible given the reality of the social, political, and economic context of the 1950s. Parks could not bring the new creation into its fullness, but through faith in Christ, she helped to fan the flames of change. In her life and actions, Rosa Parks entered into the practice of Godbearing in the world, bearing the image of God within, bearing faithful witness in her words and deeds, and bearing with God the suffering of others. Parks demonstrates that anyone can become a Godbearer, participating in radical relationship with God; we need only look at the flag-draped coffin beneath the rotunda to imagine the possibilities.

The witness of Rosa Parks—and the other Godbearers we have encountered—enables us to return, in chapter 5, to the present moment and the spiritual malaise of the U.S. churches. We are reminded that "evangelism" has misrepresented the good news of God in Christ in the Holy Spirit in the world. But we are offered the possibility of reorientation toward life giving and receiving relationships, and we can become sharers and bearers of the gospel in our world today.

five OPENING AGAIN TO LIFE

In the opening pages of this book, we argued that the church in the United States has lost its way, following the map of "evangelistic" practices. Numbers or various forms of empirical data have often become the measure of "success" or the means by which we evaluate the faithfulness of a denomination, congregation, or community. We have megachurches overflowing with purpose-driven people who seek the blessing of their best life now, preferring fulfillment to the future hope of God's new creation. We have little brown churches in the vale struggling to keep their doors open and clinging to that old rugged cross, desperate to remain true to the pure "faith of the fathers." Whatever the form of the church, at heart, our task is the same. We have lost our way toward God in Christ in the Holy Spirit and substituted the cheap grace of self-justification for the costly grace of radical relationship. We have taken God's name in vain to pursue worldly gain: unrestrained and unrelenting consumption, individualism that leads us to self-glorification or self-renunciation, imperialism that seeks to rule over all the nations of the world as if a benevolent big brother. But the way of the gospel resists these temptations and turns increasingly toward the life-centered good news found in Jesus Christ and the scriptural witnesses. The gospel calls us to be transformed by the revolutionary power of grace and to express in tangible ways the fullness of life abundant and lasting.

Although contemporary ecclesiastical life has promoted and prescribed evangelism as the answer to the decline of the church and the spirit of the times, the programs and practices of evangelism often seem to speak more with the voice of a false prophet than that of a messenger of the living God. Before God, numbers and balance sheets are without merit. We can't earn our salvation by the numbers we gather around the altar or stage from Sunday to Sunday. God isn't some denominational or church board that studies our statistics and proclaims, "Well done, good and faithful servant." Evangelism, as the sharing of the good news, is conceptually and historically significant, but in general, in our contemporary milieu, it is no longer very biblically or spiritually attuned. The word itself is misleading and has a tendency to misdirect our gifts and graces, our focus and faith, away from God and the fullness of life that is found only in and through what we are calling the practice of Godbearing as it takes shape in the world. Godbearing offers us a renewed and re-centered way of embodying and expressing the gospel.

In this last chapter, we draw our argument to a close and consider three overarching concerns of the Godbearing life as revealed in the witnesses to Jesus Christ, the Godbearing figures of scripture, and the historical persons who represent this practice of giving and receiving the fullness of life. Indeed, if we were to make any concise claim about Godbearing in the world, it is simply this: God came into the world in Jesus Christ and the Holy Spirit so that we might have life abundantly. Not some of us for the sake of some higher quality of life, but the fullness of life as intended by God for all. *Godbearing is about the manner in which we participate in the giving and receiving of life in its fullness.* Godbearing is the essence of the good news that Christ lived for us—and still lives today.

To live our lives in God is to live a life-centered existence. Although this claim sounds needlessly tautological, in fact, it presents a claim that stands in contradiction to the ways of the world and societal standards. As human beings with the free will to choose among various options within existence, our choices are frequently death-dealing ones for ourselves, for others, and for creation. When we do not choose to live our lives in God, then we are choosing the way of death for ourselves, since the fullness of life is found only in and through God in Christ in the Holy Spirit. But we often deceive ourselves into believing that our choices are God's will, when in fact, they are death-dealing, especially to others or to the created world. We pursue society's temptations and convince ourselves that having these things is God's will for us. We select scriptural passages or translations that justify our choices and make us feel good. We turn our heads and avert our eyes, believing that if we render the poor and marginalized invisible, then their diminished lives have no claim upon us.

But God sees. We can fool ourselves for only so long. We can deal death in the name of God, as Saul of Tarsus did, but our participation in sustaining and inviting brokenness will one day catch up with us. Either in this life or at the Day of Judgment, we will stand before pure Love, and God will ask us face-to-face, "Tell me, how have you lived so that others might have life abundantly?" Answering that we brought others to Christ will pale in comparison to having waded hip deep into the waters of giving and receiving life by every means possible. Even the language of "bringing someone to Christ" conveys the image of dropping a person in front of Jesus and then leaving the rest in Jesus' hands. Indeed, the uncomfortable message resounding in Matthew 25, the Letter of James, and the scriptures from beginning to end tells us it is not enough to bring someone to Jesus. If we claim to give others spiritual life or to point them toward faith, but then turn our back on their emotional, material, and physical needs, we are not in right relationship to God, self, others, or creation. We have not opened ourselves to participate in the radical relationship that follows upon faith in Christ.

To enter into the fullness of life in God is to choose the life-centered discourse of scripture and the way of Godbearing in the world. From the preceding chapters, we are able now to conclude with three basic criteria that provide some means for evaluating whether we are open to radical relationship or we continue to accept the world's deathly presumptions and attitudes that offer us and others unameliorated brokenness. The criteria that arise out of our study of scripture and history might be named briefly in terms of clothing ourselves in the attitude of openness. We are to clothe ourselves in the life of God or, as Paul writes to the Romans, to "put on the Lord Jesus Christ" (Rom. 13:14). When we accept the gift of faith in Jesus Christ, we must strip ourselves bare, removing the old clothing with which we have adorned ourselves and standing naked before God as if the first people in the proverbial Garden of Eden, no longer hiding who we really know ourselves to be. Indeed, when God calls out, "Where are you?" in Genesis 3:9, it is not as if God doesn't know the answer. Only when we allow the trappings and garments of the world to be removed and stand naked before God can we put on Jesus Christ and allow the Christ character to take shape within us. As we explore further this idea of being clothed anew in Christ, we will come to understand how each of us today might become open to Godbearing in the world.

OPENNESS TO THE WORD

Central to the Christian faith is the Word. We speak of the Word become flesh, the Word of life, the Word of God. A half century ago, Karl Barth's theology described a threefold Word of Christ, scripture, and proclamation. Each of these forms of the Word remains important to the life of faith, but for Barth, the transcendent, wholly otherness of God meant that only through God's revelation in the Word did we have any access to relationship with God. In this view, whether intended by Barth or not, the Word is figured as something that comes at us like a ball from the pitcher's hand and we wait to catch it. In other words, our role is to sit before it and receive. What is sidelined in this version of the Word—and should be reclaimed—is the Word's thoroughly dialogical quality. The Word is always in the midst of conversation and dialogue and, as we have previously suggested, it is integral to the process of giving and receiving life.

Earlier when we examined the witnesses to Jesus, the prototypical Godbearer, we discovered the dialogical nature of his teaching and, more importantly, his way of being in relationship. Throughout the gospels, Jesus is engaged in conversations with men and women from all social locations and ethnic and religious groups. Rather than forcing his Word upon others, he more often participates in an exchange that allows the other person to arrive at his or her own conclusions. This fact is particularly important when we recognize the power dynamics that are frequently at work in conversations. Even when Jesus is the "superior" according to society's norms, he does not wield that power so as to close off conversation, but instead, empowers others to join with him in sharing the Word. Similarly, the gospel of Luke suggests Jesus' mother Mary engages in conversation with an angel of God, who does not force the Word upon her, despite her powerlessness. We also noted how the different witnesses of scripture present a dialogical model demonstrating the interplay of diverse perspectives. When we read the Bible, we may privilege one voice over others, but the text itself presents the voices as a conversation without providing an instruction manual or highlighting those passages that are dominant. This sense of giving and receiving, of hearing and being heard suggests that the Word is revealed only in and through mutuality and relationship. When we are unwilling to be in conversation and to hear the other person's perspective, we are closed to the Word that can illuminate our path and transform us. As Cowan and Lee helpfully point out, "No one takes leave of a real conversation the same as when one entered into it. Our conversations create us. Conversation and risk and conversion belong together. Conversation is dangerous, therefore, to anyone unwilling to embrace or at least to accept transformation."[1]

If we are open to the Word and to the conversation it entails, then we will necessarily find ourselves located in community. This claim is basic to the Christian faith, for whenever we accept the gift of faith we become a member of the body of Christ, the community of believers. We move, at least initially, from individual existence into the possibility of radical relationship. To be in community and in genuine relationship, we open ourselves to conversation, especially conversations that can effect change deep within us. Relationship means hearing perspectives different from our own without being threatened by them. It means listening as well as sharing, giving as well as receiving the Word. In today's churches, there is often a diminishment of conversation, though this diminishment can arise out of the best of intentions. In larger churches, for example, we often self-select into small groups that are homogeneous and present little that challenges or alters our understanding of the Word of life. In smaller churches, we will sometimes cling to the way "we've always done things" and refuse to discuss new ways of being faithful to God. In reality, we isolate ourselves to avoid the risky, sometimes painful and uncomfortable process of transformation that happens in the midst of conversation. Moreover, when we isolate ourselves in one manner or another, we also minimize the opportunity to be held accountable to the transforming grace of God. We don't really want to engage the Word of God because we are comfortable just the way we are—at least, until the world's brokenness tackles us from behind.

By faith, we are called to live in radical relationship, which means opening ourselves to conversation with God, ourselves, others, and creation. As with any relationship, relationship with God involves a certain level of mutual concern; it requires us to share in both listening and speaking. Sometimes our prayer lives become little more than a monologue in which we tell God what we would like God to do. In fact, this is usually how we teach our children to pray: "God bless Mommy and Daddy, Uncle Pete and Auntie Mae, and make my teacher nicer, and please bring me a new bicycle. Amen." But the reality of prayer also mandates that we sit quietly in the presence of God and of scripture so that God might speak to us. The Word of God comes to us not in the hurricane, earthquake, or fire, but in the sheer silence (1 Kings 19:11–12). The Word of God comes to us in our inner rooms where God breathes on us like Jesus appearing to the disciples and repeating three times, "Peace be with you" (John 20).

Conversation with God also indicates that the power differential should not become a barrier in which we convince ourselves we are powerless in this relationship and can only beg God to act on our behalf. Because we are given the gift of free will, we are not simply acted upon in this relationship. Instead, God asks us to do something as well. God asks that we hear and respond, not only receiving our own life from God, but also giving life away to others. To be in relationship to God in and through the Word, we are asked to do something for God—not in order somehow to earn our salvation or status before God, but because life in God demands the giving and receiving of life. We must be willing to change and to act as givers of life in relationship to others, ourselves, and the whole of creation. We listen to our cat's meow, knowing it means she wants to be fed, and speak to her while reaching for the bag of food. We ask the dog if he wants to go for a walk or ride and, as he barks happily or excitedly at us, we gently urge him to "Sit!" while we get the leash. We strike up a conversation with a stranger at the bus stop and continue to ponder the encounter days later, having been struck by some new insight. We ask a coworker how she's doing and pause long enough to hear and respond with genuine interest. We stretch out with a friend under the shady elm swapping stories, gazing at the billowing clouds. We share a cup of steaming coffee with a neighbor, elbows propped on the table, almost close enough to touch. We read a story with our child for the hundredth time and continue to be delighted by her questions. Opening ourselves to genuine conversation means following the way of love, which is ever patient and kind and never boastful or arrogant. The way of love does not insist upon its own way, but chooses to be in dialogue. Clothed in the Word, our participation in genuine conversation becomes a practice and a gift of love. Clothed in the Word, we take our first step toward the Godbearing life.

OPENNESS TO LIVING ON THE EDGE OF THE RAFT

With the first criterion in place—that is, embracing the dialogical quality of the Word—we are led into the second step toward assessing our commitment to living as a Godbearer. If conversation leads toward transformation, then we become clothed in the process of movement rather than some false notion of stasis or arrival. It is not uncommon for people to resist change, especially when they sense that change will be painful, that it will require them to relinquish their existing comfort levels. But life in God demands that we open ourselves to transformation across time and space; we agree to be pruned in preparation for new growth to occur. For many Christians, "conversion" is a singular event to which we can point as we remember a moment of movement from brokenness to life, from turning inward to turning Godward. In a sense, conversion as a one-time event points toward fulfillment, arrival, homecoming rather than the beginning of a long journey. Thus, to speak of a conversion experience in the singular is misleading and, in reality, even riskier than the discomfort of change, since when we resist transformation, we also reject the possibility of becoming fully human in the midst of radical relationship.

Sallie McFague helps us to rethink this notion of conversion as a punctiliar event when she writes of conversion as "life on the edge of a raft."[2] She begins by helping us to understand the two common usages of "conversion": "either an abrupt change to an enthusiastic religious attitude accompanied by a highly emotional experience, or the passing over from one perspective on reality to another. The two meanings may not be unrelated, but it is the second which carries the deeper freight and more revolutionary potential."[3] McFague goes on to suggest that conversion in the latter sense is about reorientation or moving from one perspective to another, "living on the edge of a raft, disoriented, open to an unknown future, risking all one had so painstakingly put in place for oneself."[4] This sense of life as disorientation and reorientation means "we become open for the experience of transcendence; we become vulnerable to God."[5] Rather than clinging to our humanly constructed notions of reality and what matters in life, rather than trying to control our lives and destiny, rather than finding ourselves comfortable and settled, we instead become open to the life of God taking shape within us and redirecting our way in the world. Conversion is thus a lifelong process, "fraught with doubt, with ambiguity, with great discomfort, with risk" and it is a journey that demands courage.[6] By grace through faith, we let go of the world's conception of becoming and enter into the disorienting unknown. For McFague this is parabolic existence, demonstrated to us by the subversive teachings of Jesus, the stories that upend our expectations.

Yet, in this notion of opening ourselves to transcendence and the risk of reorientation, we are not suggesting that we lose our ability to act or become passive recipients of grace. To the contrary, we retain and deepen our sense of agency. No longer paralyzed by what the world might think or what it might mean for our comfortable, climate-controlled existence, we eat meat with the gentiles, denounce the colonial powers that have been the source of our livelihood, remain seated on a bus. We are freed to act courageously and boldly empowered by radical relationship and the commitment to life over death. And we are able to acknowledge the false gods we have followed and the broad paths we have tread, turning again toward the hand of grace that seeks to walk with us toward newness. As we become more open to God and learn more about ourselves in relationship to God, self, others, and creation, we enter into a process that leads us more thoroughly into the world as Godbearers who bear the renewed image of God within, bear witness to others, and bear with God the world's sufferings. We might say that we becoming increasingly inclined toward radical relationship.

To speak of inclination is to evoke a sense of movement, direction, and orientation. We duck into the wind and continue to climb the mountain of God, we stretch out our arms toward the heavens and dance with the divine, we lean our bodies nearer to someone whose life is failing them and breathe the words, "Peace be with you." We continue to run the race set before us, to see Jesus hungry and naked and to provide food and clothing, to incline our hearts to the giving and receiving of life in the face of death. Thus, saying yes to Jesus Christ does not consist in a moment's ecstasy, but in a lifetime of turning toward relationship and away from brokenness. Conversion must be understood as an ongoing process in which our deepening relationships disorient and reorient our existence, enabling the transformation that brings us closer to being fully human as God intends us to be. We find ourselves on the edge of a raft, leaning into the future with the courage that comes from faith in God in Christ in the Holy Spirit every moment that we are willing to let God lead us into new life.

OPENNESS TO THE FUTURE

Once we accept the notion that Godbearing can be identified through our openness to conversation and our openness to transformation, we encounter a third aspect of openness: openness to the future. Often, Christian faith is envisioned as leading toward some form of closure, in which we become clear on exactly what we are to believe, to do, to think, to say, and to expect through faith in Jesus Christ. Often Christians speak in terms that demand closure. We use the triumphalist language of winning and losing, of God being on our side, of who's in and who's out. We cannot ignore the criticism that Christians express kindness and love so long as we think there is a possibility of converting the other person, and once we no longer have confidence that the person will agree to confess Jesus as his or her Lord and Savior, we become closed to further relationship. We cannot sidestep the criticism that Christians are too often known by our judging than our love. Perhaps we are commanded above all else to love because from within the reality of brokenness we are more inclined to judge. We become closed to the giving and receiving of life, even as we profess to follow Jesus.

Indeed, the resurrection announces quite the opposite of closure. The resurrection is the shock of life and an open horizon and future in the face of what seemed to be death and closure. Of course, faith necessarily entails change, transformation, letting go of paths we once pursued as leading toward the good life. It means we direct our attention to the giving and receiving of life and increasingly relinquish our participation in myriad forms of brokenness. Yet, even as our path narrows when we enter into radical relationship, the reality of the resurrection as a message of hope for the future opens new possibilities before us. Death opens into life; sorrow into joy; the end into the beginning; injustice into justice; powerlessness into power. When we are open to the hope of the future rather than controlled by the lure of present fulfillment, we discover that God's promises point toward a new identity, new heavens and earth, a new creation. Ahead of us, the horizon unfolds full of the abundance of life.

But we are called by God to walk by faith and not by sight, to move confidently toward the horizon, even though we can only make out its broad contours. We are like the blind man at Bethsaida who needed to be touched by Jesus more than once because his sight remained blurred after the first attempt at healing (Mark 8:22–26). Indeed, the scriptures point us toward the horizon each time someone is miraculously healed by Jesus, since every one of those healed by Jesus continues to have blurred vision and lives, partially healed but still living in the world with its brokenness. None whom Jesus healed is alive today in the flesh—sooner or later, the blind man's eyes ceased again to see. The horizon toward which we travel remains covered with clouds like the summit of Mount Sinai. We cannot distinguish the wheat from the chaff or remove the bad fish from the net. We have no way of knowing what our resurrected body will look like or how we will be together with our loved ones. We are unable to paint a landscape of the new creation and hang it on our living room wall. We cannot discern if universal salvation is God's will, or whether those who have not confessed Christ are under God's salvific grace in much the same way as those who have chosen to follow Christ. We may argue relentlessly for our version of the "truth," angry that anyone would dare to challenge our most fiercely held and deeply comforting beliefs. But the tomb remains empty and we await Jesus' return, leaving us peering into the mystery that is God. Either we remain open to the horizon and the future that God offers, no matter how disorienting or uncomfortable it may be at any moment, or we become closed in upon ourselves and refuse to look to the future, accepting instead the lure of whatever the present might offer us. The empty tomb reminds us that we still await the completion of all things and are urged to continue faithfully toward the promised future.

BECOMING A NEW CREATION IN CHRIST

Our vision of the future remains hidden among the shadows, but in our openness to the horizon—as well as to conversation and ongoing reorientation—our attention is directed back to the present moment and the reality of putting on Jesus Christ. In radical relationship to God, we begin to understand ourselves in a new light, as a new creation, possessing a new identity quite unlike the old person who chased after false gods such as consumerism, individualism, and imperialism. We can no longer live as if God wants us to choose the temptations that Jesus rejected in the wilderness. We can no longer participate in systems that "bless" us while dealing death to countless nameless, faceless, "invisible" persons. We can no longer bring someone to Christ and then leave God to do the rest, acting like a corporate headhunter or an ambulance driver for the divine. Instead, to renew the spiritual depths in our churches means that we must take on a new identity—as did both Marys, Paul, Bartolomé de Las Casas, and Rosa Parks—and this identity is best expressed in and through the practice of Godbearing.

Godbearing can be understood as the revolutionary, subversive power of grace forming the Christ character within us and overflowing into the world in radically relational ways. No longer focused upon the standards of society that urge us to be the first, best, most, least, or lowest as a sign of favored status or blessing, we live radically related to God, self, others, and the whole of creation. Our lives begin to express the content of the gospel through giving and receiving life in its fullness, rather than participating in the painful reality of brokenness. Godbearing can be affirmed in the midst of openness to conversation, ongoing reorientation, and the horizon of the new creation.

Yet, what cannot be set aside or minimized in the openness to radical relationship is our calling to accept and embody transformation, to let go of our tendency to cling to the comfort of the old and the desires and standards of this world. The command to repent reverberates across the landscape of our contemporary society and echoes toward the horizon. We must repent, if we hope to follow

Jesus and choose the way of Godbearing in the world. Too often Christianity in the United States turns repentance into an individual admission of sin, recounting a laundry list of bad behaviors. To be sure, the scriptures and the gospel message renounce lying, cheating, stealing, adultery, murder, and the like. There is no disputing that these behaviors undermine right relationship, and that we should strive to be consistent in our denunciation of such things. But just as the communal body known as Israel was called many times to repent and turn back to God, so too the communal body known as the body of Christ, the church, is called to repent and turn back to God.

Today, our churches and our life in God are gasping for breath. We are enamored with the desires of the surrounding culture and proclaim that God desires that we be fulfilled in the here and now. Or we cling to the old rugged cross, afraid to say anything or do anything that might chase away members. Make them feel good and they will come; call them to genuine transformation and they will leave. We substitute the techniques and methods of evangelism, the simple slogans and easy way of an ecstatic moment of accepting Jesus as Lord and Savior for the risky, difficult, daily struggle against the temptations that surround us. We choose to receive life, but leave God and others to the work of giving life and condemn those who disagree with our comfortable faith. But faith in Christ is not about making more money, acquiring more possessions, exercising unlimited power, placing ourselves first, remaining silent, or staying stuck on the cross, still weeping over Jesus' death while participating daily in systems and practices that continue to deal death to others. If we open ourselves to the scriptural understanding of Godbearing as an ongoing response to grace, then we must live in the light of the resurrection and the promised return of the living God. We must, to paraphrase Joshua 24:15–23, choose this day whom we will serve, whether the other gods that seduce us to love the world's brokenness or God in Christ in the Holy Spirit, who loves us even when we turn away. And if we do choose God, then we must put away the foreign gods among us, incline our hearts to God, repent, and begin to live the life that is life-centered and inescapably relational.

Indeed, accepting faith in Christ means renouncing identity as a purely individual reality. By faith in Christ, we become part of larger reality, woven into the fabric of creation in which the harmony and radical relationship of God are the very sinews that hold us and move us. As a communal reality, as a body in radical relationship to God, ourselves, others, and the whole of creation, we must—like Bartolomé de Las Casas—turn away from living off of systems that enslave others in poverty, starvation, degradation, violence, and death. We must—like Rosa Parks—become tired enough to sit in quiet protest against the institutions that perpetuate brokenness while calling it justice. Like Jesus of Nazareth, we must be willing to turn over some tables in the temple or rub against the grain of society, even if it means the powers-that-be of this world are threatened by our words and actions. We must be willing to ride the bus to work or to learn Spanish or to demand a recycling program in our hometown. We must be willing to boycott companies that rely on cheap foreign labor in order to line the pockets of the corporate executives. We must be willing to invite the impoverished into our communities of faith, even if it means we have to tithe more of our income to support the church's ministries. To be a new creation in Christ and a member of the body of Christ means that our eyes can see beyond our divisions and brokenness to the harmony and relationship that God has promised to restore in the future. It means that we recognize the places where we can and must give away life, even as we receive it abundantly.

In the final consideration, Godbearing is not some new practice or method for renewing the church. It is the deep and powerful message of the gospel. It is the spiritual and material reality of God's grace taking shape like a child within those who are willing to risk openness and change, so that grace can overflow in the world as we become agents of life in the face of death. As human beings, we live between the cross and the resurrection, but Jesus of Nazareth, who is the content of the gospel, has shown us the way toward abundant life and a future where death shall be no more. By grace through faith, we can participate in the reality of God, giving and receiving life, growing into the Christ character in the present and pointing toward the future coming of God. Jesus Christ lived for us! Jesus Christ still lives for us today! Through Godbearing in the world we can share the gift of life with others and the whole of creation until Christ comes again.

notes

Introduction

1. My use of the terms "unchurched" and "unconnected" is a means of distinguishing between those who do not participate in a community of faith and those who do not experience or accept the reality of the living God, as these are not the same condition, though neither represents the fullness of participation in the life of God in Christ in the Holy Spirit in the world.

CHAPTER ONE: The Spirit of Our Times

1. Benton Johnson, Dean R. Hoge, and Donald A. Luidens, "Mainline Churches: The Real Reason for Decline," *First Things* 31 (March 1993), 13.

2. The terms "evangelism" and "evangelization" are generally considered to be synonymous.

3. Lyle E. Schaller, *A Mainline Turnaround* (Nashville: Abingdon, 2005), 19.

4. William C. Symonds, Brian Grow, and John Cady, "Earthly Empires," *Business Week,* 3934 (May 23, 2005), 81.

5. James B. Twitchell, "Jesus Christ's Superflock," *Mother Jones* 30:2 (Mar/Apr 2005), 4.

6. Luisa Kroll, "Megachurches, Megabusinesses," *Forbes* (September 17, 2003), online at http://www.forbes.com/2003/09/17/cz_lk_0917megachurch.html.

7. Interview with Joel Osteen by Larry King on *CNN Larry King Live* (June 20, 2005).

8. Robert D. Putnam and Lewis M. Feldstein, "Saddleback Church," *Better Together: Restoring the American Community* (New York: Simon & Schuster, 2003), 122f.

9. Ibid., 126.

10. Johnson, et al., "Mainline Churches," 16.

11. Ibid., 18.

12. William J. Abraham, *The Logic of Evangelism* (Grand Rapids: Eerdmans, 1989).

13. The technical definition of "infinity" in mathematics is far more complex. While acknowledging the risk of oversimplification in using a more philosophical understanding, it serves well for our heuristic purposes.

14. Peter Tyson, "Contemplating Infinity: A Philosophical Perspective," transcript from *Infinite Secrets,* aired on NOVA and found online at http://www.pbs.org/wgbh/nova/archimedes/contemplating.html.

15. Rodney Clapp, "Why the Devil takes Visa," *Christianity Today* 40:11 (October 7, 1996), 21.

16. Ibid.

17. Ibid., 24.

18. Ibid., 21.

19. Ibid.

20. Ibid., 25.

21. Vincent J. Miller, *Consuming Religion: Christian Faith and Practice in a Consumer Culture* (New York: Continuum, 2005), 117.

22. John Kavanaugh, "Capitalist Culture as a Religious and Educational Formation System," *Religious Education* 78:01 (Winter 1983), 54.

23. Miller, *Consuming Religion,* 119.

24. Ibid., 116.

25. Ibid., 119.

26. Ibid., 120.

27. Ibid., 128.

28. Ibid., 130.

29. Robert Bellah et al., *Habits of the Heart: Individualism and Commitment in American Life* (New York: Harper & Row, 1985), 142.

30. Bellah et al., *Habits of the Heart,* 143, and quoting Robert Coles, "Civility and Psychology" 109 *Daedalus* (Summer 1980), 137.

31. Miller, *Consuming Religion,* 86.

32. Ibid., 135.

33. See, for example, Wade Roof Clark, *A Generation of Seekers: The Spiritual Journeys of the Baby Boom Generation* (San Francisco: Harper-SanFrancisco, 1993) and *Spiritual Marketplace: Baby Boomers and the Remaking of American Religion* (Princeton, N.J.: Princeton University Press, 1999) and Charles Taylor, *Sources of the Self* (Cambridge: Harvard University Press, 1989).

34. Robert D. Putnam, *Bowling Alone: The Collapse of American Community* (New York: Simon & Schuster, 2000). Putnam's study of Saddleback Church in his follow-on work, *Better Together,* illustrates the problem of individualism as much as it offers a solution to the decline of community.
35. Taylor, *Sources of the Self,* 17.
36. Ibid., 47.
37. Ibid., 111.
38. Anthony Giddens, *Modernity and Self-Identity* (Stanford, Calif.: Stanford University Press, 1991), 5.
39. Ibid., 14.
40. Taylor, *Sources of the Self,* 491.
41. Ibid., 18.
42. Justo L. González, *Mañana: Christian Theology from a Hispanic Perspective* (Nashville: Abingdon, 1990), 83–84.
43. Jack Nelson-Pallmeyer, *Saving Christianity from Empire* (New York: Continuum, 2005), 98.
44. United Nations Environment Programme, "North America's Environment," Nairobi, Kenya, 2002, xiv.
45. Ibid., xv.
46. United Nations, *The Inequality Predicament: Report on the World Social Situation 2005* (United Nations, 2005), 108.
47. Kofi A. Annan, *In Larger Freedom: Towards Development, Security and Human Rights for All* (United Nations, 2005), 2.
48. United Nations, *The Inequality Predicament,* 71.
49. Ibid., 72.
50. Ibid., 71.
51. See Myra Jehlen, *American Incarnation: The Individual, the Nation, and the Continent* (Cambridge, Mass: Harvard University Press, 1986).
52. Robert N. Bellah, "Righteous Empire," *Christian Century* 120:5 (March 8, 2003), 23. cf. Bellah, "The New American Empire: The Likely Consequences of the 'Bush Doctrine,'" Anxious About Empire, ed. Wes Auram (Grand Rapids: Brazos Press, 2005), 23.
53. Nelson-Pallmeyer, *Saving Christianity,* 7.
54. Quoted in Ron Suskind, "Without a Doubt," *New York Times Magazine* (October 17, 2004), 51.
55. Nelson-Pallmeyer, *Saving Christianity,* 8ff.
56. Howard Zinn, "The Power and the Glory: Myths of American Exceptionalism," *Boston Review* (Summer 2005).
57. Ibid.
58. Richard A. Horsley, *Jesus and Empire* (Minneapolis: Fortress Press, 2003), 78.

59. Ibid.

60. Ibid., 98.

61. Ibid., 99.

62. Ibid., 105.

63. Ronald Rolheiser, *The Holy Longing: The Search for a Christian Spirituality* (New York: Doubleday, 1999), 3.

64. Ibid., 7.

CHAPTER TWO: Why "Evangelism" Isn't the Answer

1. Mark A. Noll, *American Evangelical Christianity: An Introduction* (Oxford: Blackwell, 2001), 13.

2. Ibid.

3. Karl Barth, *Evangelical Theology: An Introduction,* trans. Grover Foley (New York: Holt, Rinehart and Winston, 1963). He writes: "The qualifying attribute 'evangelical' recalls both the New Testament and at the same time the Reformation of the sixteenth century. . . . The expression 'evangelical,' however cannot and should not be intended and understood in a confessional [manner]. . . . [Evangelical] theology intends to apprehend, to understand, and to speak of the God of the Gospel, in the midst of the variety of all other theologies and (without any value-judgment being implied) in distinction from them." *Evangelical Theology,* 5f.

4. Noll, *American Evangelical Christianity,* 13.

5. Ibid.

6. Mark A. Noll, *The Rise of Evangelicalism: The Age of Edwards, Whitefield, and the Wesleys* (Downers Grove, Ill: InterVarsity Press, 2003), 19. See David W. Bebbington, *Evangelicalism in Modern Britain: A History from the 1730s to the 1980s* (London: Unwin Hyman, 1989).

7. Noll, *The Rise of Evangelicalism,* 19.

8. The political commitments of some prominent evangelicals, notably Jim Wallis, often run counter to the political pronouncements of the Religious Right. There is a growing sense that U.S. evangelicals are becoming increasingly fractured. Thus, we are reminded that categories remain fluid and of heuristic value. See Michael Luo, "Evangelicals Debate the Meaning of 'Evangelical,'" *New York Times,* Sunday April 16, 2006, WK 5.

9. Of course, not all Protestant denominations that relate to eighteenth-century Anglo-U.S. revivalism fall into Noll's category of "evangelical" Protestant churches—a point that further clouds the discussion. The survey was conducted by the Angus Reid Group of Toronto in October 1996. Noll, *American Evangelical Christianity,* 30–43.

10. Noll, *American Evangelical Christianity,* 37.

11. Ibid., 32–33.
12. Ibid., 34.
13. My assumption here is that theological diversity is to be valued and dialogue from significantly distinct perspectives is not only to be cultivated, but also enables us to search more faithfully for the fullness of God's word and presence as it takes shape in our world today.
14. Some significant departures from the evangelical approach come from a liberation perspective: Cheri DiNovo, *Qu(e)erying Evangelism,* (Cleveland: Pilgrim Press, 2005); Orlando E. Costas, *Liberating News: A Theology of Contextual Evangelization* (Grand Rapids: Eerdmans, 1989); Mortimer Arias, *Announcing the Reign of God: Evangelization and the Subversive Memory of Jesus,* reprinted by Academic Renewal Press (Minneapolis: Fortress Press, 1984), among others.
15. See, for example, José Serra, "The Other September 11," *Dissent* (Winter 2004): 85–89.
16. Abraham, *The Logic of Evangelism* (Grand Rapids: Eerdmans, 1989), 96.
17. Ibid., 98, 103–04.
18. Ibid., 105.
19. Ibid., 101.
20. Delores Williams, *Sisters in the Wilderness: The Challenge of Womanist God-Talk* (Maryknoll, N.Y.: Orbis Books, 1993).
21. Arias, *Announcing the Reign of God,* 89.
22. Ibid., 90–91.
23. Ibid., 92.
24. Ibid.
25. Ibid., 93–94.
26. Ibid., 98.
27. Abraham, *The Logic of Evangelism,* 149.
28. Ibid.
29. Ibid., 96.
30. David J. Bosch, *Transforming Mission: Paradigm Shifts in Theology and Mission* (Maryknoll, N.Y.: Orbis Books, 1991), 48, and quoting the phrase of J. C. Hoekendijk in *Kirche und Volk in der deutschen Missionswissenschaft* (Munich: Chr. Kaiser Verlag, 1967), 245.
31. C. René Padilla, *Mission Between the Times: Essays on the Kingdom* (Grand Rapids: Eerdmans, 1985), 143.
32. Ibid., 145.
33. Bosch, *Transforming Mission,* 51.
34. Ibid., 43.

35. Ibid., 44.
36. Ibid., 153–57.
37. Padilla, *Mission Between the Times,* 149.
38. This comment in no way denies the ways in which many churches transfer funds to poorer churches, but to note that it is a transfer of funds and not a melding of believers into one heterogeneous body.
39. Padilla, *Mission Between the Times,* 167, and footnote 43, quoting Clowney, "The Missionary Flame of Reformed Theology," in *Theological Perspectives on Church Growth,* ed. Harvey M. Conn (Nutley, N.J.: Presbyterian and Reformed Publishing, 1976), 145.
40. Abraham, *The Logic of Evangelism,* 44. Abraham's phrase is far from original. Bosch cites the "famous adage" on page 81 of Stephen Neill's *Creative Tension* (London: Edinburgh House Press, 1959): "If everything is mission, nothing is mission." See Bosch, *Transforming Mission,* 511.
41. Abraham, *The Logic of Evangelism,* 212.
42. Ibid., 229.
43. Although I do not find his thesis well supported by the evidence, especially when considering the range of usage in the New Testament writings, his chronological examination of the words provides a useful summary.
44. Craig A. Evans, "'Preacher' and 'Preaching': Some Lexical Observations," *Journal of the Evangelical Theological Society* 24/4 (December 1981): 316.
45. Michael Green, *Evangelism in the Early Church,* rev. ed. (Grand Rapids: Eerdmans, 1970, 2003), 87.
46. Ibid.
47. Ibid., 80.
48. Ibid.
49. Evans, "'Preacher' and 'Preaching,'" 317.
50. Ibid., 82.
51. Green, *Evangelism in the Early Church,* 76. See James Barr, *The Semantics of Biblical Language* (London: Oxford University Press, 1961).
52. Green, *Evangelism in the Early Church,* 91.
53. Ibid., 108.
54. Ibid., 112.
55. Langdon Gilkey, *Maker of Heaven and Earth* (New York: Anchor Books, 1965), 221.
56. Evans, "'Preacher' and 'Preaching,'" 319.
57. Mendell Taylor, *Exploring Evangelism* (Kansas City: Beacon Hill Press, 1964), 19. Taylor goes on to note that a second book was published in 1888 by Arthur T. Pierson, *Evangelistic Work in Principle and Practice.*

58. Bosch, *Transforming Mission,* 409.

59. *Oxford English Dictionary Online,* 2nd ed. 1989, "gospel."

60. Bosch, *Transforming Mission,* 409.

61. For an excellent discussion of the relationship between mission and evangelism, see Bosch, *Transforming Mission,* 409–20. Bosch concludes that evangelism should be seen as an integral dimension of mission.

62. See, for example, Emilio Castro, "Liberation, Development, and Evangelism: Must We Choose in Mission?," *Occasional Bulletin of Missionary Research* (2 July 1978), 87–90; Samuel Escobar, *The New Global Mission* (Downers Grove, Ill: InterVarsity Press, 2003); and Bosch, *Transforming Mission.*

63. My argument assumes that evil is real and not simply attributable to God by pointing to the limited understanding of human beings as in classical theism.

64. Of course, the Pauline witness to the resurrection of the "body" is complicated by our ability to translate from Greek the meaning of "soma."

65. Escobar, *The New Global Mission,* 144.

66. Ibid., 145–46.

67. Ibid., 146f.

68. Arias, *Announcing the Reign of God,* 107.

69. Ibid., 108.

70. Ibid., 112–13, quoting Gustavo Gutiérrez, *A Theology of Liberation* (Maryknoll, N.Y.: Orbis Books, 1981), 204–05. See also Emilio Castro, "Evangelism and Social Justice," *Ecumenical Review* 20:2 (April 1968), 146–50, and C. René Padilla, "The Fullness of Mission," *Occasional Bulletin of Missionary Research* (3 January 1979), 6–11.

71. Serene Jones' discussion of essentialism in *Feminist Theory and Christian Theology* (Minneapolis: Fortress, 2000) provides a basic overview of the issue.

72. Sallie McFague, *The Body of God* (Minneapolis: Fortress, 1993), 14.

73. Elisabeth Moltmann-Wendel, *I Am My Body: A Theology of Embodiment* (New York: Continuum, 1995), 104. See also, Kathryn Tanner, *Jesus, Humanity, and the Trinity* (Minneapolis: Fortress, 2001), 112f., where she discusses the problem associated with spiritualizing eternal life.

74. See "Mission/Evangelization," *Encyclopedia of Christian Theology,* ed. Jean-Yves Lacoste (New York: Routledge, 2004), Routledge Reference Resources online.

75. From Paulos Mar Gregorios, "The Witness of the Churches: Ecumenical Statements on Mission and Evangelism," *Ecumenical Review* 40 (Jul/Oct 1988), 359–66.

76. Taylor, *Exploring Evangelism,* 312.

77. Ibid., 444–45. In his *History of Evangelism,* Paulus Scharpff indicates that "Weekly reports on evangelism continued to come out regularly in *The Evangelist,* a periodical founded in New York in 1831" (though the appendix contains a chronology of events that lists the founding in 1830). Scharpff does not attribute the inception of this magazine to the work of Charles Finney, but to the many Congregationalist and Presbyterian revivalists at work throughout New England. *History of Evangelism,* trans. Helga Henry (Grand Rapids: Eerdmans, 1966), p. 104ff.

CHAPTER THREE: Jesus, the Prototypical Godbearer

1. Harold J. Recinos, *Who Comes in the Name of the Lord?: Jesus at the Margins* (Nashville: Abingdon, 1997), 39.

2. Larry W. Hurtado, *Lord Jesus Christ: Devotion to Jesus in Earliest Christianity* (Grand Rapids: Eerdmans, 2003), 263.

3. R. S. Sugirtharajah, *The Bible and the Third World: Precolonial, Colonial, and Postcolonial Encounters* (Cambridge: Cambridge University Press, 2001), 276.

4. Dietrich Bonhoeffer, *Christ the Center* (New York: Harper & Row, 1966, 1978), 34.

5. Valerie Saiving, "The Human Situation: A Feminine View," *Journal of Religion,* 40/2 (April 1960), 100–12.

CHAPTER FOUR: Following Jesus

1. See, for example, Jane Schaberg, *The Illegitimacy of Jesus: A Feminist Theological Interpretation of the Infancy Narratives* (San Francisco: Harper and Row, 1987).

2. Jürgen Moltmann, *The Way of Jesus Christ: Christology in Messianic Dimensions,* trans. Margaret Kohl (San Francisco: HarperSanFrancisco, 1990).

3. Kallistos Ware, "Mary Theotokos in the Orthodox Tradition," *Epiphany Journal* (Winter 1989), 51.

4. Robert W. Jenson, "A Space for God," *Mary, Mother of God,* ed. Carl E. Braaten and Robert W. Jenson (Grand Rapids: Eerdmans, 2004), 51.

5. Marie Asaad, "Text: Luke 1.26–55, Theme: The Magnificat," *Feminist Theology from the Third World: A Reader,* ed. Ursula King (Maryknoll, N.Y.: Orbis Books, 1994), 207.

6. Richard Covington, "A Long Miscast Outcast," in "Women of the Bible: Provocative New Insights," special collector's edition, *U.S. News & World Report:* (2006), 66.

7. Jane Schaberg, "Magdalene Christianity," *On the Cutting Edge: The Study of Women in Biblical Worlds,* ed. Jane Schaberg, Alice Bach, and Esther Fuchs (New York: Continuum, 2004), 198.

8. Carla Ricci, *Mary Magdalene and Many Others: Women Who Followed Jesus* (Minneapolis: Fortress Press, 1994), 135.

9. Ibid., 138.

10. Here we should note that the name of Paul emerges in his first encounter with a Roman following his reorientation and reflects a cross-cultural adaptation.

11. Frederick Buechner, *Telling the Truth: The Gospel as Tragedy, Comedy, and Fairy Tale* (San Francisco: Harper & Row, 1977), 8.

12. Richard A. Horsley, "General Introduction," *Paul and Empire,* ed. Horsley (Harrisburg, Pa.: Trinity Press International, 1997), 6.

13. Ibid., 8.

14. Bartolomé de Las Casas, *Historia de las Indias* (1.3, cs. 3–7, 1757–1774). Quoted in Luis N. Rivera-Pagán, "A Prophetic Challenge to the Church: The Last Word of Bartolomé de las Casas," inaugural lecture as Henry Winters Luce Professor in Ecumenics and Mission, delivered on April 9, 2003, at Princeton Theological Seminary. Online at http://www.lascasas.org/Rivera_Pagan.htm.

15. The historical information about Las Casas is drawn largely from Paolo G. Carozza, "From Conquest to Constitutions: Retrieving a Latin American Tradition of the Idea of Human Rights," *Human Rights Quarterly* 25:2 (May 2003), and David Orique, O.P., "Bartolomé de Las Casas: A Brief Outline of His Life and Labor," online at http://www.lascasas.org/manissues.htm.

16. Carozza, "From Conquest to Constitutions," 289.

17. Ibid., 290.

18. Orique, "Bartolomé de Las Casas," 2.

19. Ibid.

20. Carozza, "From Conquest to Constitutions," 289.

21. Ibid., 290.

22. Bartolomé de Las Casas, "Brief Account of the Devastation of the Indies" (1542).

23. Rivera-Pagán, "A Prophetic Challenge to the Church."

24. Ibid.

25. Carozza, "From Conquest to Constitutions," 290.

26. Rosa Parks, *Quiet Strength: The Faith, the Hope, and the Heart of a Woman who Changed a Nation,* with Gregory J. Reed (Grand Rapids: Zondervan, 1994), 16.

27. Ibid., 70.
28. Ibid., 16.
29. Ibid., 64.
30. Ibid., 30.
31. Ibid., 17.
32. Ibid., 27.

CHAPTER FIVE: Opening Again to Life

1. Michael A. Cowan and Bernard J. Lee, *Conversation, Risk, and Conversion: The Inner and Public Life of Small Christian Communities* (Maryknoll, N.Y.: Orbis Books, 1997), 1.
2. Sallie McFague, "Conversion: Life on the Edge of a Raft," *Interpretation* 32:3 (July 1978), 255–68.
3. Ibid., 255.
4. Ibid., 257.
5. Ibid., 258.
6. Ibid., 259.

index of authors and subjects

Abraham, William J., 8, 44–58, 75
Arias, Mortimer, 51–52
Augustine, 16, 90, 93
Barth, Karl, 46, 73–74, 143
Bonhoeffer, Dietrich, 89, 109
Bosch, David, 54, 68, 69
brokenness, 78
Carozza, Paolo, 133
Christ character, 25, 34, 77, 79–81
Clapp, Rodney, 13–14
Cone, James, 46
consumerism, 12–17, 18, 100
conversation, 95–96, 104, 143–46
conversion, 71–72, 146–48
cross, crucifixion, 107–112
cultural consciousness, 45, 46–47, 57
dialogue (see conversation)
empire (see imperialism)
encomienda system, 132–33
Escobar, Samuel, 71
evangelicalism (defined), 41–43
evangelism, 39–40, 48, 58; definitions of, 49, 58, 63, 69
Evans, Craig, 59–60, 67
Finney, Charles, 14, 42, 74
future, 148–50
Gilkey, Langdon, 65
Godbearing, 76, 81–82, 84–85, 141, 150
González, Justo, 26–27, 36
gospel, 25, 48, 59, 62–67
  etymology of, 68
Green, Michael, 59–60, 62
historical consciousness, 45–46, 57
Horsley, Richard, 31–32, 129–130
identity, 16, 20–22, 54–55, 57
imperialism, 26–32, 100–101
incarnation, 63, 65, 70, 72, 103
individualism, 17–26, 99
Jenson, Robert, 115
life, giving and receiving, 80, 91, 96–104, 111–12, 141, 145
Luther, Martin, 23
McFague, Sallie, 72, 146–47
Miller, Vincent, 14–16
misdirection, 16
mission, 70–73
Moltmann, Jürgen, 114
Moltmann-Wendel, Elisabeth, 72
new creation, 49, 65, 107, 150
Noll, Mark, 41–43
numbers, empirical data, 10–12, 38–39, 140–41
openness, 40, 96, 142–150
Osteen, Joel, 7–8
Padilla, C. René, 54–55
radical relationship, radical relationality, 63–65, 80–81, 99, 104–6,

Recinos, Harold, 86
reorientation, 37, 57, 79, 146–47
repentance, 151
resurrection, 106, 120–22, 148–49
Ricci, Carla, 122
risk, 89, 116, 147
Rolheiser, Ronald, 33–34
Saiving, Valerie, 110
Schaberg, Jane, 114
scripture, 31, 48–49, 85–89, 143
seduction, 15–16
suffering, 106–112
Sugirtharajah, R.S., 88
Taylor, Charles, 21–22
transcendence, 50–51, 143, 147
transformation, 88, 146–148, 150–51
triumphalism, 57–58
Ware, Kallistos, 114
witness (testimony), 62, 94–106
Warren, Rick, 8, 19
Williams, Delores, 51
Word, 88–89, 143–46

index of scripture

Genesis
- 2–3 65
- 3:9 142

Exodus
- 33:17–23 64

Joshua
- 24:15–23 151

1 Kings
- 19:11–12 145

Psalms
- 34:8 98
- 51:16–17 108

Isaiah
- 42 60

Ezekiel
- 37 90

Hosea
- 6:6 108

Matthew
- 1:19 116
- 2:16 92
- 4:1–11 . . . 9–10, 12, 17, 26, 32
- 5 . . . . 95, 97–98
- 5:3 60
- 6–7 97–101
- 8:5 96
- 11:5 60
- 14:23 93
- 15:21–28 . . . . 47, 111
- 25 . . . . 105, 106, 142
- 27:54 . . . . 90, 92
- 28 . . . . 48, 121

Mark
- 7:24–30 . . . . 47, 111
- 8:22–26 149
- 8:27 95
- 10:17 96
- 15:34 111
- 16 121

Luke
- 1:26–38 . . . . . . 115, 116, 117
- 1:46–55 . . . . 117, 118
- 2:2 121
- 4:1–13 9
- 4:18 60
- 4:34 92
- 5:12–14 111
- 6:20 60
- 7:22 60
- 8:1–3 120
- 9:18 120
- 10:25–37 101–2
- 18:18–30 101
- 20 96
- 24:4–7 120

John
- 3:13–18 103
- 3:16 . . . . 27, 103
- 4 . . . . 96, 111
- 4:29 92
- 14:5–8 91
- 17:1–26 93
- 20 145
- 20:11–18 121

Acts
2:44 55
4:32 55
8:3 125
9:1 125
13:9–11 126
19:8–9 126
20 126
21 127
22:15 127
24:10 127
26:20 127
27:34 127
28:8 127
Romans
7:15 94
8:35–39 128
10:15 61
13:14 142
15:16 61
15:19 61
15:20–21 61
15:26 129
1 Corinthians
5:9–13 129
6:1–11 129
9:14 61
10:14–22 129
13 . . . . 67, 128
13:22 64
14:33b–36 125
15:1–2 61
2 Corinthians
9 129
Galatians
2:2 61
3:28 54
6:2 130
Philippians
1:5 61
2:1–11 128
1 Thessalonians
2:2 61
3:6 61
James 95, 142